Extending Kubernetes

Elevate Kubernetes with Extension Patterns, Operators, and Plugins

Onur Yilmaz

Apress®

Extending Kubernetes: Elevate Kubernetes with Extension Patterns,
Operators, and Plugins

Onur Yilmaz
Berlin, Germany

ISBN-13 (pbk): 978-1-4842-7094-3
https://doi.org/10.1007/978-1-4842-7095-0

ISBN-13 (electronic): 978-1-4842-7095-0

Copyright © 2021 by Onur Yilmaz

Managing Director, Apress Media LLC: Welmoed Spahr
Acquisitions Editor: Aditee Mirashi
Development Editor: Laura Berendson
Coordinating Editor: Aditee Mirashi

Cover designed by eStudioCalamar

Cover image designed by Freepik (www.freepik.com)

Distributed to the book trade worldwide by Springer Science + Business Media New York, 1 New York Plaza, Suite 4600, New York, NY 10004-1562, USA. Phone 1-800-SPRINGER, fax (201) 348-4505, e-mail orders-ny@springer-sbm.com, or visit www.springeronline.com. Apress Media, LLC is a California LLC and the sole member (owner) is Springer Science + Business Media Finance Inc. (SSBM Finance Inc.). SSBM Finance Inc. is a **Delaware** corporation.

For information on translations, please e-mail booktranslations@springernature.com; for reprint, paperback, or audio rights, please e-mail bookpermissions@springernature.com.

Apress titles may be purchased in bulk for academic, corporate, or promotional use. eBook versions and licenses are also available for most titles. For more information, reference our Print and eBook Bulk Sales web page at http://www.apress.com/bulk-sales.

Any source code or other supplementary material referenced by the author in this book is available to readers on GitHub via the book's product page, located at www.apress.com/978-1-4842-7094-3. For more detailed information, please visit http://www.apress.com/source-code.

Printed on acid-free paper

For my wife Nursin and my daughter Ece
for their incredible support

Table of Contents

About the Author

Onur Yilmaz is a senior software engineer at a multinational enterprise software company. He is a Certified Kubernetes Administrator (CKA) and works on Kubernetes and cloud management systems as a keen supporter of cutting-edge technologies. Furthermore, he is the author of multiple books on Kubernetes, Docker, serverless architectures, and cloud-native continuous integration and delivery. In addition, he has one master's and two bachelor's degrees in the engineering field.

About the Technical Reviewer

Erkan Erol is a software engineer and Certified Kubernetes Application Developer (CKAD). He has been working on the lifecycle management of applications on Kubernetes and developing operators for 3.5 years.

Introduction

The future is in the skies.

—Mustafa Kemal Ataturk, Founder of Turkish Republic

In recent years, applications have become smaller and more self-governing with the microservices paradigm shift. Furthermore, they are built, tested, and deployed as containers with less overhead and flexibility. Thus, if you aim to develop the applications of the future, you need to aim for the clouds and containers. However, the management of distributed applications in a scalable, reliable, and flexible way is not straightforward. You need a well-architectured abstraction layer between applications and the clouds. Kubernetes has become the de facto orchestrator for cloud-native applications running in the containers with its open architecture and industry adoption.

Kubernetes is a complex but open system with well-designed extension points and plugins. It is possible to extend Kubernetes by implementing the APIs in a cloud-native way and make it work for your custom requirements and infrastructure. This book is a comprehensive guide for understanding the extension patterns and discovering the extension plugins for Kubernetes. In this book, you will learn the state-of-the-art extension patterns and extension points of Kubernetes in depth with real-life use cases and examples. You will have a comprehensive overview of all possible aspects of Kubernetes, starting from end user to the fully automated controller development. Also, the book focuses on creating applications that not only work on Kubernetes but also interact and operate Kubernetes itself.

INTRODUCTION

This book is for a wide range of audience, including, but not limited to, software engineers, developers, DevOps engineers, cloud security analysts, architects, and managers who have Kubernetes in their short- and long-term plans. However, this is not a starter's guide to containers, cloud providers, or Kubernetes. It is expected to have an introductory knowledge and hands-on experience on Kubernetes to grasp the content fully and follow up the activities.

In the following chapters, Kubernetes API and extension points with respective design patterns will be covered with their theoretical background, hands-on activities, and exercises. At the end of the book, you will be more enthusiastic about the future of Kubernetes and how you will extend the Kubernetes to enrich its ecosystem.

CHAPTER 1

Introduction

Life is like an onion; you peel it off one layer at a time, and sometimes you weep.

—Carl Sandburg
American poet, biographer, journalist,
and editor with three Pulitzer Prizes

Kubernetes is like an onion. You peel it off one layer at a time, and sometimes you weep, check your YAML file, and read more documentation.

Kubernetes is a complex system. This first chapter will start with a short history of Kubernetes and how it has grown to a complex system. Although it already has many layers, it is also extensible with additional layers. This chapter will also discuss how to configure a Kubernetes system, its extension patterns, and points. At the end of this chapter, you will grasp the complexity of Kubernetes and its capabilities.

Let's start with a short recap of Kubernetes history and its features.

Kubernetes Recap

Kubernetes is an open source system for managing containerized applications. The name originates from Greek with the meaning of **helmsman**. So, it is not wrong to say that Kubernetes is the tool to help you find *Moby Dick* in the stormy oceans of containers and microservices.

© Onur Yilmaz 2021
O. Yilmaz, *Extending Kubernetes*, https://doi.org/10.1007/978-1-4842-7095-0_1

Google open-sourced Kubernetes in 2014, and it was the accumulated experience of running production workloads in containers over decades. In 2015, Google announced the Kubernetes project's handover to the Cloud Native Computing Foundation (CNCF).[1] CNCF has over 500 members,[2] including the world's most giant public cloud and enterprise software companies and over a hundred innovative startups. The foundation is a vendor-neutral home for many of the fastest-growing projects including *Kubernetes*, *Prometheus*, and *Envoy*.

Kubernetes is currently one of the most popular open source projects with nearly 3000 contributors, more than 1000 pull requests, and 2000 open issues. The repository (Figure 1-1) is available at GitHub under the name kubernetes/kubernetes.[3]

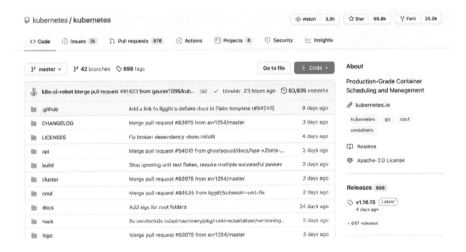

Figure 1-1. *Kubernetes repository*

---

[1] www.cncf.io

[2] www.cncf.io/about/members

[3] https://github.com/kubernetes/kubernetes

There is an enormous amount of open issues to resolve, and if you want to dive into the open source world to contribute, the community is also one of the most welcoming ones. Now let's tackle one level more and check what we mean by a Kubernetes system.

Kubernetes is designed to run on the clusters. A Kubernetes cluster consists of nodes, and the containerized applications run on these nodes.

We can divide a Kubernetes system logically into two: **the control plane and worker nodes**. The control plane manages the worker nodes and the cluster's workload, whereas the worker nodes run the workload. In Figure 1-2, you can see how the components of a Kubernetes cluster are tied together.

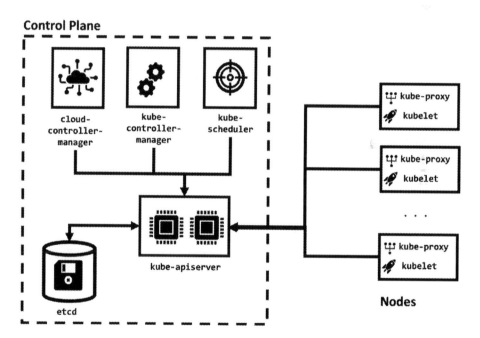

Figure 1-2. *Kubernetes components*

Control Plane Components

The control plane is the **brain** of a Kubernetes cluster to make decisions, detect events, and respond if required. For instance, the control plane is expected to give scheduling decisions of pods to worker nodes, identify failed nodes, and reschedule new pods to ensure scalability.

Control plane components can run on any node in the Kubernetes cluster; however, it is a typical approach to save some nodes for only control plane components. This approach separates the workloads from control plane components in a cluster and makes it easier to operate nodes for scaling up and down or maintenance.

Now, let's review each control plane component and their importance to the cluster.

kube-apiserver

Kubernetes API is the front end of the control plane, and the kube-apiserver exposes it. kube-apiserver can scale horizontally by running multiple instances to create a highly available Kubernetes API.

etcd

etcd is an open source distributed key-value store, and Kubernetes stores all its data in it. The state of the cluster and changes are saved in etcd by only kube-apiserver, and it is possible to extend the etcd horizontally.

kube-scheduler

Kubernetes is a container orchestration system, and it needs to assign the containerized applications to nodes. kube-scheduler is responsible for scheduling decisions by taking into account resource requirements, available resources, hardware and policy constraints, affinity rules, and data locality.

kube-controller-manager

One of the key design concepts of Kubernetes is the controller. Controllers in Kubernetes are control loops for watching the state of the cluster and make changes when needed. Each controller interacts with Kubernetes API and tries to move the current cluster state to the desired shape. In this book, you will not only be familiar with the native Kubernetes controllers but also learn how to create new controllers to implement new capabilities. `kube-controller-manager` is a set of core controllers for a Kubernetes cluster.

cloud-controller-manager

Kubernetes is designed to be a platform-independent and portable system. Therefore, it needs to interact with cloud providers to create and manage the infrastructure such as nodes, routes, or load balancers. The `cloud-controller-manager` is the component to run controllers specific to the cloud provider.

Node Components

Node components are installed to every worker node in a Kubernetes cluster. Worker nodes are responsible for running the containerized applications. In Kubernetes, containers are grouped into a resource named as *pod*. `kube-scheduler` assigns pods to the nodes, and node components ensure they are up and running.

kubelet

`kubelet` is the agent running in each node. It fetches the specification of the pods that are assigned to the node. It then interacts with the container runtime to create, delete, and watch containers' status in the pod.

kube-proxy

Containerized applications operate like running in a single network while running inside a Kubernetes cluster. kube-proxy runs on every node as a network proxy and connects applications. It also maintains network rules for inside and outside cluster network communication.

In a production environment, control plane components run over multiple nodes to provide fault tolerance and high availability. Similarly, the number of worker nodes scales with the workload and resource requirements. On the other hand, it is possible to create more portable Kubernetes systems running on a single node inside Docker containers or virtual machines for development and testing environments. Throughout the book, we will create both production-ready and single-node Kubernetes clusters and see them in action. In the following section, we will focus on configuring the Kubernetes system to understand its capabilities.

Configuring the Kubernetes Cluster

You can restrain or liberate a Kubernetes cluster by two broad approaches: configuration and extensions. In the configuration approach, you can change flags, configuration files, or API resources. This section will focus on configuring the Kubernetes, and then we will move our focus to extensions in the rest of the book.

The control plane and node components have their flags and configuration files defined in the reference documentation.[4] Also, it is possible to get your hands dirty and check them by using Docker images. Let's start with kube-apiserver and check its flags as shown in Listing 1-1.

---

[4]https://kubernetes.io/docs/reference/command-line-tools-reference/

Listing 1-1. kube-apiserver flags

```
$ docker run -it --rm k8s.gcr.io/kube-apiserver:v1.19.0 kube-
apiserver --help

The Kubernetes API server validates and configures
data for the api objects which include pods, services,
replicationcontrollers, and others. The API Server services
REST operations and provides the frontend to the cluster's
shared state through which all other components interact.

Usage:
  kube-apiserver [flags]

Generic flags:

    --advertise-address        ip
    The IP address on which to advertise the apiserver to
    members of the cluster. ...
    ...
    --cors-allowed-origins    strings
    List of allowed origins for CORS, comma separated.
    ...
```

The command-line output is enormous, with nearly 150 flags for the kube-apiserver binary. However, there is one flag which every cluster admin needs to know: --feature-gates. Feature gates are a set of key and value pairs to enable alpha or experimental Kubernetes features. It is available in every Kubernetes component and reachable through its help. Let's check for kube-scheduler this time as shown in Listing 1-2.

Listing 1-2. kube-scheduler flags

```
$ docker run -it --rm k8s.gcr.io/kube-scheduler:v1.19.0 kube-
scheduler --help 2>&1 |grep -A 250 feature-gates

--feature-gates      mapStringBool
A set of key=value pairs that describe feature gates for alpha/
experimental features. Options are:
        APIListChunking=true|false (BETA - default=true)
        APIPriorityAndFairness=true|false (ALPHA - default=false)
        APIResponseCompression=true|false (BETA - default=true)
        AllAlpha=true|false (ALPHA - default=false)
        AllBeta=true|false (BETA - default=false)
        ...
```

There are 85 feature gate options for the kube-scheduler in the particular version, so the output is also very long. Experimental features in Kubernetes need to go to alpha and beta before graduation or depreciation. You can track the features' status in the official reference documentation[5] with their default value, stage, start, and end versions as in Figure 1-3.

---

[5]https://kubernetes.io/docs/reference/command-line-tools-reference/feature-gates/

Feature	Default	Stage	Since	Until
AnyVolumeDataSource	false	Alpha	1.18	
APIListChunking	false	Alpha	1.8	1.8
APIListChunking	true	Beta	1.9	
APIPriorityAndFairness	false	Alpha	1.17	
APIResponseCompression	false	Alpha	1.7	
AppArmor	true	Beta	1.4	
BalanceAttachedNodeVolumes	false	Alpha	1.11	
BoundServiceAccountTokenVolume	false	Alpha	1.13	
CPUManager	false	Alpha	1.8	1.9
CPUManager	true	Beta	1.10	

Figure 1-3. *Feature gates*

In managed Kubernetes systems such as Amazon Elastic Kubernetes Service (EKS) or *Google Kubernetes Engine (GKE)*, it is impossible to edit the flags of control plane components. However, there are options to enable all alpha features in Google Kubernetes Engine[6] with `--enable-kubernetes-alpha` flag similar to `--feature-gates=AllAlpha=true`. It is valuable to use alpha clusters for early testing and validation of new features.

The configuration of Kubernetes enables designing tailor-made clusters. Therefore, it is essential to grasp the configuration parameters of the control plane and node components. However, configuration parameters only allow you to tune what is already inside the Kubernetes. In the next section, we will expand the boundaries of Kubernetes with extensions.

---

[6]`https://cloud.google.com/kubernetes-engine/docs/how-to/creating-an-alpha-cluster`

Kubernetes Extension Patterns

Kubernetes design is centered on Kubernetes API. All Kubernetes components such as kube-scheduler and clients such as kubectl operate interacting with the Kubernetes API. Likewise, the extension patterns are designed to interact with the API. However, unlike the clients or Kubernetes components, extension patterns enrich the capabilities of Kubernetes. There are three well-accepted design patterns to extend the Kubernetes.

Controller

Controllers are loops for managing at least one Kubernetes resource type. They check the spec and status fields of the resource and take action if required. In the spec field, the desired state is defined, whereas the status field represents the actual state. We can illustrate the flow of a controller as in Figure 1-4.

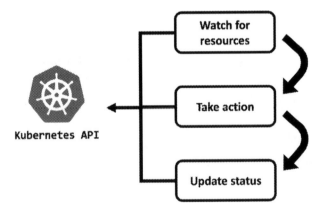

Figure 1-4. *Controller pattern in Kubernetes*

Let's take a real controller from Kubernetes and try to understand how they operate. CronJob is a Kubernetes resource to enable running Jobs on a repeating schedule. Job is another Kubernetes resource that runs one or more pods and ensures them to terminate successfully. CronJob has a controller defined in the Go package k8s.io/kubernetes/pkg/controller/cronjob. You can create an example CronJob resource like the following.

Listing 1-3. Example CronJob resource

```
apiVersion: batch/v1beta1
kind: CronJob
metadata:
  name: example
spec:
  schedule: "*/1 * * * *"
  jobTemplate:
    spec:
      template:
        spec:
          containers:
          - name: hello
            image: busybox
            args:
            - /bin/sh
            - -c
            - date; echo Hello from the Kubernetes CronJob
          restartPolicy: OnFailure
```

The desired state is in the spec field, and there are two important sections: schedule and jobTemplate. schedule defines the interval, and it is every minute for example CronJob. The jobTemplate field has the Job definition with containers to execute.

We can expect the CronJob controller to watch CronJob resources and create Jobs when their schedules occur. The source code is relatively long, but we can highlight some important points. The syncOne function in the cronjob_controller.go is responsible for creating the Jobs and updating a single CronJob instance's status.

Listing 1-4. CronJob controller

```
jobReq, err := getJobFromTemplate(cj, scheduledTime)
...
jobResp, err := jc.CreateJob(cj.Namespace, jobReq)
...
klog.V(4).Infof("Created Job %s for %s", jobResp.Name, nameForLog)
recorder.Eventf(cj, v1.EventTypeNormal, "SuccessfulCreate",
"Created job %v", jobResp.Name)

...

// Add the just-started job to the status list.
ref, err := getRef(jobResp)
if err != nil {
    klog.V(2).Infof("Unable to make object reference for job
    for %s", nameForLog)
} else {
    cj.Status.Active = append(cj.Status.Active, *ref)
}
cj.Status.LastScheduleTime = &metav1.Time{Time: scheduledTime}
if _, err := cjc.UpdateStatus(cj); err != nil {
    klog.Infof("Unable to update status for %s (rv = %s):
    %v", nameForLog, cj.ResourceVersion, err)
}
...
```

When you deploy the sample CronJob resource, you can see both the updated status and created Job resources in the cluster as shown in Listing 1-5.

Listing 1-5. CronJob in action

```
$ kubectl apply -f cronjob_example.yaml
cronjob.batch/example created

$ kubectl get cronjob example -o yaml

apiVersion: batch/v1beta1
kind: CronJob
metadata:
  ...
  name: example
  namespace: default
  ...
spec:
        concurrencyPolicy: Allow
        failedJobsHistoryLimit: 1
        jobTemplate:
            ...
  schedule: '*/1 * * * *'
  successfulJobsHistoryLimit: 3
  suspend: false
status:
  active:
  - apiVersion: batch/v1
    kind: Job
    name: example-1598968200
    namespace: default
    resourceVersion: "588"
    uid: e4603eb1-e2b3-419f-9d35-eeea9021fc34
  lastScheduleTime: "2020-09-01T13:50:00Z"
```

```
$ kubectl get jobs
NAME                    COMPLETIONS    DURATION    AGE
example-1598968200      1/1            4s          119s
example-1598968260      1/1            4s          59s
example-1598968320      1/1            3s          8s
```

> **Note**   The source code for the CronJob controller is available on
> GitHub: `https://github.com/kubernetes/kubernetes/`
> `tree/master/pkg/controller/cronjob`.

Controllers offer a robust extension pattern with the help of custom resources in Kubernetes. It is possible to extend the Kubernetes API by defining custom resources and manage them by controllers. In Chapter 4, we will both extend the Kubernetes API and write custom controllers to implement this design pattern.

Webhook

Webhook is an HTTP callback to send event notifications and get back the results. In Kubernetes API, it is possible to validate some events such as authorization, validation, or resource mutation by external webhooks. Kubernetes queries an outside REST service to process such events. We can illustrate the flow of the requests as in Figure 1-5.

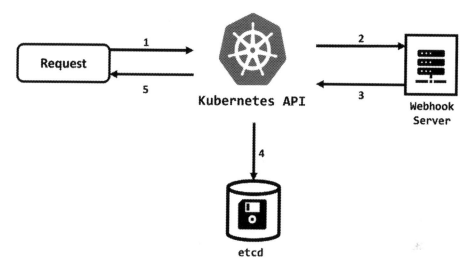

Figure 1-5. *Flow of request in Kubernetes*

When a new user wants to connect to the Kubernetes API, the request
is packaged and sent to the defined webhook address and checks for the
response. The webhook server could send the following data like in Listing 1-6
if the user is authorized.

Listing 1-6. Authorization webhook response

```
{
  "apiVersion": "authorization.k8s.io/v1beta1",
  "kind": "SubjectAccessReview",
  "status": {
    "allowed": true
  }
}
```

Similarly, if the user wants to change a resource in Kubernetes API,
it is possible to query the webhook server to validate the change. When
the webhook backend accepts the change by sending the following data
similar to Listing 1-7, Kubernetes API will apply the changes.

Listing 1-7. Change webhook response

```
{
  "apiVersion": "admission.k8s.io/v1",
  "kind": "AdmissionReview",
  "response": {
    "uid": "<value from request.uid>",
    "allowed": true
  }
}
```

Webhook backend are easy to follow design patterns to extend software applications. However, webhooks add a point of failure to the system and need great attention during the development and operation.

Binary Plugin

In the binary plugin pattern, Kubernetes components execute third-party binaries. Node components such as kubelet or client programs such as kubectl utilize this pattern since it requires extra binaries on host systems For instance, kubectl executes third-party binaries with the function in Listing 1-8.

Listing 1-8. kubectl binary plugin handling

```
// Execute implements PluginHandler
func (h *DefaultPluginHandler) Execute(executablePath string,
cmdArgs, environment []string) error {

        // Windows does not support exec syscall.
        if runtime.GOOS == "windows" {
                cmd := exec.Command(executablePath, cmdArgs...)
                cmd.Stdout = os.Stdout
                cmd.Stderr = os.Stderr
```

```
        cmd.Stdin = os.Stdin
        cmd.Env = environment
        err := cmd.Run()
        if err == nil {
                os.Exit(0)
        }
        return err
    }

    // invoke cmd binary relaying the environment and args given
    ..
    return syscall.Exec(executablePath, append([]
    string{executablePath}, cmdArgs...), environment)
}
```

The Go function Execute calls the external binary and captures its input and output to the command line. In the following chapters, you will create similar plugins and see binary plugin pattern in action.

Note   Source code of the kubectl is available at GitHub: https://github.com/kubernetes/kubernetes/blob/ master/pkg/kubectl/cmd/cmd.go.

As software engineering design patterns, extension patterns are accepted and repeatable solutions to common problems in Kubernetes. If you have similar obstacles, the patterns help implement solutions. However, it should be kept in mind that neither design patterns nor extension patterns are silver bullets. They should be treated as methods to extend the Kubernetes systems. With multiple components and API endpoints, Kubernetes has a broad set of open points to the extensions. In the following section, we will have a more technical overview of these extension points in Kubernetes.

Kubernetes Extension Points

Kubernetes is an open system, but it is not like every Kubernetes component is a LEGO brick to plug in new stuff. There are particular extension points that you can extend the skills of a Kubernetes system. There are five principal groups of extension points with their implemented patterns and working area:

- **kubectl Plugins**: kubectl is the indispensable tool of the users interacting with the Kubernetes API. It is possible to extend kubectl by adding new commands to its CLI. The kubectl plugins implement the binary plugin extension pattern, and users need to install them in their local workspace.

- **API Flow Extensions**: Each request to Kubernetes API passes through steps: authentication, authorization, and admission controls. Kubernetes offers an extension point to each of these steps with webhooks.

- **Kubernetes API Extensions**: Kubernetes API has various native resources such as pods or nodes. You can add custom resources to the API and extend it to work for your new resources. Furthermore, Kubernetes has controllers for its native resources, and you can write and run your controllers for your custom resources.

- **Scheduler Extensions**: Kubernetes has a control plane component, namely, kube-scheduler, to assign the workloads over the cluster nodes. Also, it is possible to develop custom schedulers and run next to the kube-scheduler. Most of the schedulers follow the controller extension pattern to watch the resources and take action.

- **Infrastructure Extensions**: Node components interact with the infrastructure to create cluster networks or mount volumes to the containers. Kubernetes has the extension points for networking and storage by the designated Container Network Interface (CNI) and Container Storage Interface (CSI). The extension points in infrastructure follow the binary plugin extension pattern and require the executables installed on the nodes.

We have grouped the extension points based on their functionality and the implemented extension pattern. In the following chapters of the book, we will cover each group in depth. You will not only learn the extension points and their technical background but also create them and run in the clusters.

Key Takeaways

- Kubernetes is a complex system.

- You can logically divide a Kubernetes cluster into two: the control plane and node components.

- Kubernetes components have a rich set of configuration options.

- There are three extension patterns for extending the Kubernetes: controller, webhook, and binary plugin.

- Kubernetes components and its design allow many open points for extension: kubectl, API flow, Kubernetes API, scheduler, and infrastructure.

In the following chapter, we will start with the first extension point: kubectl plugins. We will create new plugins for kubectl and use the custom commands to enrich its capabilities.

CHAPTER 2

kubectl Plugins

We shape our tools, and thereafter our tools shape us.

—Marshall McLuhan
Media scholar and critic

Command-line tools are the Swiss Army knives of the developers. You can connect to backend systems, run complex commands, and automate your daily tasks with them. The official command-line tool for Kubernetes is kubectl. As the god of gates Janus in mythology, kubectl is the god of entrances into the cluster. It lets you create workloads, manage resources, and check statuses by communicating with Kubernetes API. In this chapter, we will focus on extending the kubectl by writing plugins. At the end of this chapter, you will develop and install new plugins into kubectl and run custom commands.

Let's start by installing the gods of the Kubernetes API gateways to your local workstation.

kubectl Installation and Usage

kubectl is the client tool to communicate with the Kubernetes API. Therefore, it is good to have a kubectl version exactly or close to the Kubernetes API version. Otherwise, it is possible to have incompatible API requests and failed operations. Source code of kubectl is a part of the

© Onur Yilmaz 2021
O. Yilmaz, *Extending Kubernetes*, https://doi.org/10.1007/978-1-4842-7095-0_2

official Kubernetes repository, and its releases are jointly managed with the Kubernetes releases. However, you need to check the kubernetes/kubectl[1] repository in Figure 2-1 for the issues related to kubectl.

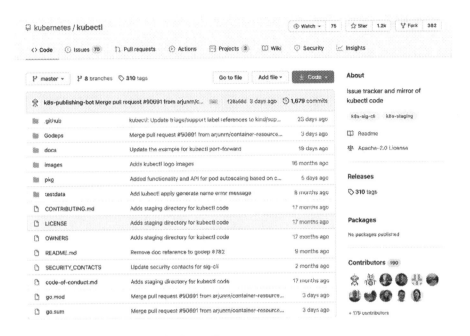

Figure 2-1. *Kubernetes kubectl repository*

The installation of kubectl is fairly straightforward since it is a single-binary application. You need first to download the binary from the release repository for your operating system as shown in Listing 2-1.

Listing 2-1. Downloading kubectl binary

```
# Linux
curl -LO https://storage.googleapis.com/kubernetes-release/
release/v1.19.0/bin/linux/amd64/kubectl
```

---

[1]https://github.com/kubernetes/kubectl

```
# macOS
curl -LO https://storage.googleapis.com/kubernetes-release/
release/v1.19.0/bin/darwin/amd64/kubectl
```

Then you need to make the binary executable.

Listing 2-2. Executable kubectl binary

```
chmod +x ./kubectl
```

Finally, you need to move the binary into your PATH.

Listing 2-3. Moving kubectl binary

```
sudo mv ./kubectl /usr/local/bin/kubectl
```

You can test the kubectl with the following command in Listing 2-4.

Listing 2-4. kubectl version check

```
kubectl version --client
Client Version: version.Info{Major:"1", Minor:"19",
GitVersion:"v1.19.0", GitCommit:"e19964183377d0ec2052d1f1
fa930c4d7575bd50", GitTreeState:"clean", BuildDate:"2020-
08-26T14:30:33Z", GoVersion:"go1.15", Compiler:"gc",
Platform:"darwin/amd64"}
```

The command prints the client version of kubectl, which is v1.19.0.
In the following exercise, you will create a local Kubernetes cluster and
continue with more complex kubectl commands interacting with the
cluster.

EXERCISE: STARTING A LOCAL KUBERNETES CLUSTER

Although Kubernetes is a container management system for large clouds, it is possible to create single-instance Kubernetes clusters locally. `minikube` is the recommended and officially supported way of creating single-node clusters. It is mostly used for development and testing purposes.

In this exercise, you will install `minikube` and start a new Kubernetes cluster.

1. Download the binary of minikube according to your operating system:

   ```
   # Linux
   curl -LO https://storage.googleapis.com/minikube/
   releases/latest/minikube-linux-amd64

   # macOS
   curl -LO https://storage.googleapis.com/minikube/
   releases/latest/minikube-darwin-amd64
   ```

2. Install the binary to the path:

   ```
   # Linux
   sudo install minikube-linux-amd64 /usr/local/bin/minikube

   # macOS
   sudo install minikube-darwin-amd64 /usr/local/bin/
   minikube
   ```

3. Start a local cluster with minikube:

   ```
   $ minikube start --kubernetes-version v1.19.0
   ☺ minikube v1.14.1 on Darwin 10.15.6
   +᠅ Automatically selected the docker driver
   🍴 Starting control plane node minikube in cluster minikube
   🐳 Pulling base image ...
   🔥 Creating docker container (CPUs=2, Memory=9000MB) ...
   ```

🐋 Preparing Kubernetes v1.19.0 on Docker 19.03.8 ...
𝒫 Verifying Kubernetes components...
🌟 Enabled addons: storage-provisioner, default-storageclass
🏃 Done! kubectl is now configured to use "minikube" by
    default

The simplicity of Kubernetes operations is packed into the single command of the `minikube start`. It downloads the images, starts control plane components, enables addons, and verifies the cluster components. In the last step, it configures `kubectl` to connect to the cluster created by `minikube`.

You have a Kubernetes cluster and a client tool. Now, it is time to have fun with Kubernetes by deploying applications, scaling them, and checking their statuses.

Usage of kubectl is based on the following syntax in Listing 2-5.

Listing 2-5. kubectl syntax

```
kubectl [command] [TYPE] [NAME] [flags]
```

command specifies the operation, such as creating, getting, describing, or deleting that you want to execute against Kubernetes API. You can list all the commands by running kubectl --help. It lists all the commands grouped by their functionality and details like in Listing 2-6.

Listing 2-6. kubectl help output

```
$ kubectl --help
kubectl controls the Kubernetes cluster manager.

 Find more information at: https://kubernetes.io/docs/
reference/kubectl/overview/
```

Basic Commands (Beginner):
```
  create        Create a resource from a file or from stdin.
  expose        Take a replication controller, service,
                deployment or pod and expose it as a new
                Kubernetes Service
  run           Run a particular image on the cluster
  set           Set specific features on objects
```

Basic Commands (Intermediate):
```
  explain       Documentation of resources
  get           Display one or many resources
  edit          Edit a resource on the server
  delete        Delete resources by filenames, stdin,
                resources and names, or by resources and label
                selector
```

. . .

TYPE specifies the type of the Kubernetes API resource such as pods, deployments, or nodes. It is possible to list the supported API resources on Kubernetes API with the following command in Listing 2-7.

Listing 2-7. kubectl API resources

```
$ kubectl api-resources --output=name
bindings
componentstatuses
configmaps
endpoints
events
limitranges
namespaces
nodes
persistentvolumeclaims
```

```
persistentvolumes
pods
podtemplates
replicationcontrollers
```

It is a long list with more than 50 resources supported currently in Kubernetes API.

NAME specifies the name of the resource to execute the command on it, the operations. If you do not specify a NAME, the commands are executed for all the resources in the TYPE.

flags are the optional variables for commands such as --namespace or --kubeconfig. You can list the options that can be passed to any command with kubectl options as shown in Listing 2-8.

Listing 2-8. kubectl options output

```
$ kubectl options
The following options can be passed to any command:
...
--cluster='': The name of the kubeconfig cluster to use
--context='': The name of the kubeconfig context to use
...
--kubeconfig='': Path to the kubeconfig file to use for CLI
requests.
-n, --namespace='': If present, the namespace scope for this
CLI request
...
--token='': Bearer token for authentication to the API server
...
-v, --v=0: number for the log level verbosity
```

You can run kubectl <command> --help to get more information such as options, usage, and examples on a given command. Considering the high number of resources and commands, kubectl is a tool packed with numerous actions. It is advised to get your hands dirty with kubectl by trying different commands. kubectl is almost exclusively the single-entry point to the cluster for deployment, status tracking, and troubleshooting. In the following exercise, you will use the most common kubectl commands to get used to it before developing extensions.

EXERCISE: GETTING STARTED WITH KUBECTL

In this exercise, you will use kubectl to interact with the Kubernetes cluster.

1. Start with checking the version of your client tool and the API server:

```
$ kubectl version
Client Version: version.Info{Major:"1", Minor:"19",
GitVersion:"v1.19.0", GitCommit:"e19964183377d0ec2052d1f1
fa930c4d7575bd50", GitTreeState:"clean", BuildDate:"2020-
08-26T14:30:33Z", GoVersion:"go1.15", Compiler:"gc",
Platform:"darwin/amd64"}
Server Version: version.Info{Major:"1", Minor:"19",
GitVersion:"v1.19.0", GitCommit:"e19964183377d0ec2052d1f1
fa930c4d7575bd50", GitTreeState:"clean", BuildDate:"2020-
08-26T14:23:04Z", GoVersion:"go1.15", Compiler:"gc",
Platform:"linux/amd64"}
```

It shows that both the client and the server have the version 1.19.0.

2. Check the nodes available in the cluster:

```
$ kubectl get nodes
NAME     STATUS ROLES  AGE VERSION
minikube Ready  master 88s v1.19.0
```

Nodes are also a resource type in Kubernetes, and the command is to retrieve them from the Kubernetes API. You will have one node since you are running a `minikube` cluster.

3. Create a deployment with the following command:

```
$ kubectl create deployment my-first-deployment
--image=nginx
deployment.apps/my-first-deployment created
```

This command creates a resource type of deployment with the name `my-first-deployment` using the image `nginx`.

4. Check the status of the deployment created in Step 3:

```
$ kubectl get deployment my-first-deployment
NAME                     READY   UP-TO-DATE   AVAILABLE AGE
my-first-deployment  1/1     1                 1              16s
```

This command retrieves the resource with its name. The deployment has one ready instance available.

5. Scale the deployment to five instances:

```
$ kubectl scale deployment/my-first-deployment
--replicas=5
deployment.apps/my-first-deployment scaled
```

This is a special command to scale the number of instances of the resource provided. The `--replicas` flag specifies the requested replica count.

6. Check the pods after scale-up:

```
$ kubectl get pods
NAME                            READY   STATUS    RESTARTS   AGE
my-first-deployment-....-26xpn  1/1     Running   0          13s
```

```
my-first-deployment-...-87fcw    1/1    Running   0          13s
my-first-deployment-...-b7nzv    1/1    Running   0          2m45s
my-first-deployment-...-kxg2w    1/1    Running   0          13s
my-first-deployment-...-wmg92    1/1    Running   0          13s
```

As expected, there are now five pods, and the last four ones are created after the first one.

7. Clean the deployment with the following command:

```
$ kubectl delete deployment my-first-deployment
deployment.apps "my-first-deployment" deleted
```

Your CLI environment has a new member, and you have started discovering its capabilities. Now, it is time to go one step further and extend its skills. In the following section, we will continue with the plugin design to add custom commands to kubectl.

kubectl Plugin Design

Core kubectl commands are essential for interacting with the Kubernetes API. Plugins extend the kubectl with new subcommands for new custom features. kubectl extensions implement the binary plugin approach. As in the binary plugin pattern, kubectl executes third-party applications as extensions. There are three main rules for plugin binaries:

- Executable

- Anywhere on the user's PATH

- Begin with kubectl-

These three rules are based on how kubectl discovers the plugins. Let's have a look at the source code of plugin handling in kubectl.

Listing 2-9. Plugin handler in kubectl

```
// Lookup implements PluginHandler
func (h *DefaultPluginHandler) Lookup(filename string) (string,
bool) {
    for _, prefix := range h.ValidPrefixes {
        path, err := exec.LookPath(fmt.Sprintf("%s-%s",
        prefix, filename))
        if err != nil || len(path) == 0 {
    continue
    }
    return path, true
        }
        return "", false
    }
}
```

Note   Source code of the DefaultPluginHandler is available at https://github.com/kubernetes/kubernetes/blob/master/pkg/kubectl/cmd/cmd.go.

DefaultPluginHandler checks for the executables in the path starting with the ValidPrefix, kubectl. Therefore, any binary named kubectl-my-first-plugin or kubectl-whoami in the PATH environment variable is an appropriate kubectl plugin. The plugin names are interpreted as subcommands, such as the binary with the name kubectl-whoami for kubectl whoami command. Thus, kubectl will check whether there are any commands in native implementation and then the plugins as shown in Figure 2-2.

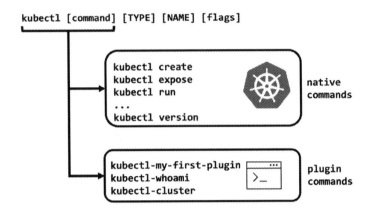

Figure 2-2. kubectl command handling

Let's have a look at how the plugins are executed in kubectl.

Listing 2-10. kubectl binary plugin handling

```
// Execute implements PluginHandler
func (h *DefaultPluginHandler) Execute(executablePath string,
cmdArgs, environment []string) error {

    // Windows does not support exec syscall.
    if runtime.GOOS == "windows" {
        cmd := exec.Command(executablePath, cmdArgs...)
        cmd.Stdout = os.Stdout
        cmd.Stderr = os.Stderr
        cmd.Stdin = os.Stdin
        cmd.Env = environment
        err := cmd.Run()
        if err == nil {
            os.Exit(0)
        }
        return err
    }
```

```
// invoke cmd binary relaying the environment and args given
  ..
  return syscall.Exec(executablePath, append([]
  string{executablePath}, cmdArgs...), environment)
}
```

Note   Source code of the DefaultPluginHandler is available at
https://github.com/kubernetes/kubernetes/blob/
master/pkg/kubectl/cmd/cmd.go.

DefaultPluginHandler has an Execute function with the inputs of
the executable path, arguments, and environment variables. The function
passes these variables to the third-party binary, which is the plugin. In
Windows, it connects the standard input and output to the command and
then executes it. In Linux and macOS, the function uses syscall on the
operating system level with the arguments and environment variables.

Now, it is time to add a new custom command to the kubectl by
creating the plugin.

Create Your First kubectl Plugins

You can list the available plugins with the kubectl plugin commands
locally.

Listing 2-11. Installed plugins

```
$ kubectl plugin list

error: unable to find any kubectl plugins in your PATH
```

There are no plugins found locally by kubectl. Now, create a file
named kubectl-whoami with the following content.

Listing 2-12. Plugin code

```
#!/bin/bash

kubectl config view --template='{{ range .contexts }}{{ if eq
.name "'$(kubectl config current-context)'" }}User: {{ printf
"%s\n" .context.user }}{{ end }}{{ end }}'
```

Move the file to a folder in your PATH environment variable and make it executable.

Listing 2-13. Plugin installation

```
sudo chmod +x ./kubectl-whoami
sudo mv ./kubectl-whoami /usr/local/bin
```

Now, rerun the kubectl plugin list command.

Listing 2-14. Installed plugins

```
$ kubectl plugin list
The following compatible plugins are available:

/usr/local/bin/kubectl-whoami
```

It shows that kubectl can discover the plugin. Let's test it and see it in action.

Listing 2-15. kubectl whoami plugin

```
$ kubectl whoami
User: minikube
```

There are two critical points about running the last command. The first point is that kubectl whoami is an extended command not available in the native implementation. However, with the extension capabilities, you can run a custom subcommand. The second point is that it is possible to retrieve information and interfere with the operations of kubectl now.

In the following exercise, you will create a kubectl prompt command to show the current Kubernetes cluster and the username in the bash prompt.

EXERCISE: KUBERNETES BASH PROMPT

Dealing with one Kubernetes cluster is easy, but it becomes cumbersome when it becomes tens of clusters in a daily routine. It is helpful to know the current cluster and the user in the terminal bash prompt not to make critical mistakes. We will have a string displayed before each command with the (user @ cluster) information.

1. Create a file with the name kubectl-prompt with the following content:

```
#!/bin/bash

currentContext=$(kubectl config current-context)
prompt="(%s @ %s) > "
template="{{ range .contexts }}{{ if eq .name
\"$currentContext\" }}{{ printf \"$prompt\" .context.user
.context.cluster}}{{ end }}{{ end }}"
kubectl config view --template="$template"
```

The script checks for all the contexts in the kubeconfig and retrieves the cluster and username fields.

2. Move the file to a folder in PATH environment variable and make it executable:

```
sudo chmod +x ./kubectl-prompt
sudo mv ./kubectl-prompt /usr/local/bin
```

3. Test the plugin with the following command:

```
$ kubectl prompt
(minikube @ minikube) >
```

4. Set the prompt environment variable:

```
$ export PS1=$(kubectl prompt)
(minikube @ minikube) >
```

From now on, every terminal command will have the prompt available. It will always be on your sight which cluster and user are in control.

Plugins extend the kubectl and help you achieve more while interacting with the Kubernetes clusters. It is expected to have similar difficulties while operating the clusters, which leads to developing similar plugins. In the following section, the focus will be on plugin repository for kubectl and how to use it.

Plugin Repository: krew

Kubernetes community has a kubectl plugin manager named krew. The plugin manager helps to discover, install, and update open source and community-maintained plugins. Currently, there are more than 100 plugins distributed on krew. Therefore, it is noteworthy to check the plugin repository before creating a new one. It is already possible someone in the Kubernetes community has developed the same functionality and distributed it.

Let's start installing the krew, a kubectl plugin itself, and discover some repository plugins. Run this command in the terminal to download krew.

Listing 2-16. Downloading krew

```
curl -fsSLO "https://github.com/kubernetes-sigs/krew/releases/
latest/download/krew.tar.gz"
tar zxf krew.tar.gz
```

Now, install the binary accordingly to the operating system.

Listing 2-17. Downloading krew

```
# Linux
./krew-linux_amd64 install krew
# macOS
./krew-darwin_amd64 install krew

Adding "default" plugin index from https://github.com/
kubernetes-sigs/krew-index.git.
Updated the local copy of plugin index.
Installing plugin: krew
Installed plugin: krew
\
 | Use this plugin:
 | kubectl krew
 | Documentation:
 | https://krew.sigs.k8s.io/
 | Caveats:
 | \
 | | krew is now installed! To start using kubectl plugins, you
     need to add
 | | krew's installation directory to your PATH:
 | |
```

```
|  | * macOS/Linux:
|  | - Add the following to your ~/.bashrc or ~/.zshrc:
|  | export PATH="${KREW_ROOT:-$HOME/.krew}/bin:$PATH"
|  | - Restart your shell.
|  |
|  | * Windows: Add %USERPROFILE%\.krew\bin to your PATH
     environment variable
|  |
|  | To list krew commands and to get help, run:
|  | $ kubectl krew
|  | For a full list of available plugins, run:
|  | $ kubectl krew search
|  |
|  | You can find documentation at
|  | https://krew.sigs.k8s.io/docs/user-guide/quickstart/.
|  /
/
```

Finally, add the krew installation directory to the path.

Listing 2-18. Path expansion

```
export PATH="${KREW_ROOT:-$HOME/.krew}/bin:$PATH"
```

Now, we can test it by calling as a kubectl plugin.

Listing 2-19. kubectl krew output

```
$ kubectl krew
krew is the kubectl plugin manager.
You can invoke krew through kubectl: "kubectl krew [command]..."
```

Usage:
```
kubectl krew [command]
```

Available Commands:
```
help        Help about any command
index       Manage custom plugin indexes
info        Show information about an available plugin
install     Install kubectl plugins
list        List installed kubectl plugins
search      Discover kubectl plugins
uninstall   Uninstall plugins
update      Update the local copy of the plugin index
upgrade     Upgrade installed plugins to newer versions
version     Show krew version and diagnostics
```

Flags:
```
-h, --help      help for krew
-v, --v Level   number for the log level verbosity
```

Use "kubectl krew [command] --help" for more information about a command.

It is now possible to search, install, and upgrade plugins managed by krew. An up-to-date list of the plugins is available on the krew website with the name, description, and GitHub popularity as shown in Figure 2-3.

Kubectl plugins available

Below you will find the list of kubectl plugins distributed on the centralized krew-index. To install these plugins on your machine:

1. Install Krew
2. Run kubectl krew install <PLUGIN_NAME> to install a plugin via Krew.

Name	Description	Repository
access-matrix	Show an RBAC access matrix for server resources	stars 655
advise-psp	Suggests PodSecurityPolicies for cluster.	stars 246
allctx	Run commands on contexts in your kubeconfig	stars 1
apparmor-manager	Manage AppArmor profiles for cluster.	stars 8
auth-proxy	Authentication proxy to a pod or service	stars 33
bd-xray	Run Black Duck Image Scans	stars 0
bulk-action	Do bulk actions on Kubernetes resources.	stars 17
ca-cert	Print the PEM CA certificate of the current cluster	stars 100
capture	Triggers a Sysdig capture to troubleshoot the running pod	stars 61
cert-manager	Manage cert-manager resources inside your cluster	stars 6.4k

Figure 2-3. *krew plugin list*

Let's assume you are running a web application in Kubernetes, and it has a service in front of the instances. To access and test the app, you need to reach the service endpoint. Luckily, the Kubernetes community has a plugin for this task. open-svc is the kubectl plugin to open the specified service URL in the browser through a local proxy server. You can install it via krew.

Listing 2-20. Installing open-svc plugin

```
$ kubectl krew install open-svc
Updated the local copy of plugin index.
Installing plugin: open-svc
Installed plugin: open-svc
\
 | Use this plugin:
 | kubectl open-svc
 | Documentation:
 | https://github.com/superbrothers/kubectl-open-svc-plugin
/
WARNING: You installed plugin "open-svc" from the krew-index
plugin repository.
    These plugins are not audited for security by the Krew
    maintainers.
    Run them at your own risk.
```

Note   If you have not enabled the Kubernetes dashboard for your cluster, you can run `minikube dashboard` to install it.

Now, let's open the Kubernetes dashboard by using the `kubectl open-svc` plugin.

Listing 2-21. open-svc plugin in action

```
$ kubectl open-svc kubernetes-dashboard -n kubernetes-dashboard
Starting to serve on 127.0.0.1:8001
Opening service/kubernetes-dashboard in the default browser...
```

The command should open the dashboard in the browser like in Figure 2-4.

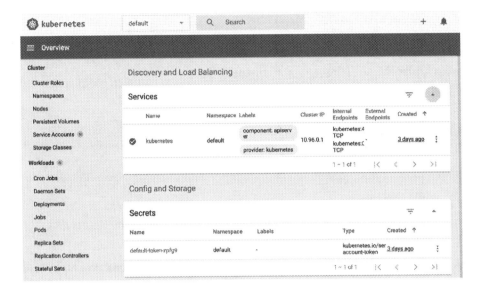

Figure 2-4. *Kubernetes dashboard*

It is just a couple of commands to install new plugins from the repository and start using them. Therefore, it is useful to check what has already been developed by the community before creating it from scratch.

Key Takeaways

- kubectl is the official client to interact with the Kubernetes API.

- Native kubectl commands are essential to operate Kubernetes clusters.

- It is possible to extend kubectl with new commands by creating plugins.

- kubectl plugins are third-party binaries, and they are executed by kubectl.

- There is a community-maintained plugin repository for kubectl, named krew.

In the following chapter, we will continue with API flow extensions and learn how to extend the flow with authentication, authorization, and admission controls.

CHAPTER 3

API Flow Extensions

It's OK to have your eggs in one basket as long as you control what happens to that basket.

> —Elon Musk
> Business magnate,
> industrial designer, and engineer

Kubernetes is the secure, reliable, and extendible home for cloud-native applications. Kubernetes API flow makes it possible to authenticate requests, decide on authorization, and pass through admission steps. The flow makes Kubernetes a protected environment while letting you define what is allowed or not. In this chapter, we will focus on extending the Kubernetes API flow and intervene with our custom decisions. At the end of this chapter, you will have a confident view of API flow and hands-on experience with the extension webhooks.

Let's start with a summary of Kubernetes API flow and its extension points.

Kubernetes API Flow

You can connect and use Kubernetes API using kubectl, client libraries, or directly sending REST requests. Every request to the API goes through authentication, authorization, and several admission control stages. All

© Onur Yilmaz 2021
O. Yilmaz, *Extending Kubernetes*, https://doi.org/10.1007/978-1-4842-7095-0_3

three stages offer extension points by webhooks and will be covered in this chapter. The flow and extension points can be illustrated in Figure 3-1.

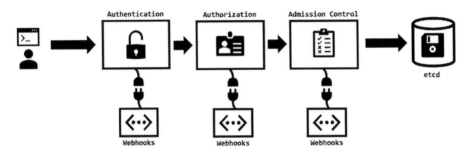

Figure 3-1. *Kubernetes API flow*

Authentication

Authentication is the first stage to validate the identity of the incoming API requests. Kubernetes uses client certificates, bearer tokens, basic auth, and authentication plugins to review the requests. In addition, it is capable of running multiple authenticators at the same time. The prevalent Kubernetes installation is expected to have the following:

- Service account tokens for the service account users

- At least one other method such as client certificates, bearer tokens, or basic auth for user authentication

You can extend the authentication mechanisms by adding a webhook authenticator to verify bearer tokens. Kubernetes will post a JSON request to the remote service, which acts as your webhook service. In the remote service, you will validate the token and decide to allow the request or not.

Authorization

Authorization is the second stage to determine whether the user can read, write, or update API resources. Authorization modules in Kubernetes check the user, group, HTTP verb, resource, and namespace attributes of the requests to verify them. Like authentication, it is possible to use multiple authorization modules such as attribute-based access control (ABAC), role-based access control (RBAC), and webhooks. You can extend the authorization by adding new webhook modules. Your custom webhook services receive the HTTP POST request with the access review data. After the evaluation, the webhook service sends back the response as allowed or not.

Admission Control

The third and the last stage for incoming requests is the admission control modules. An admission controller is a code to intercept requests coming to the Kubernetes API server after authentication and authorization but before persistence to storage. Similar to the previous stages, it is possible to run multiple admission controllers in sequence. However, there are two main differences between the earlier stages. The first one is that admission controllers are not applied for simply GET requests to read objects. The second difference is that these modules can modify requests and related entities. Thus, they can validate spec values such as container images or set default values such as CPU requests.

There are various admission controllers already packaged into kube-apiserver and enabled or disabled according to the Kubernetes version. Let's check the list of controllers from the kube-apiserver binary directly:

Listing 3-1. kube-apiserver plugin listing

```
$ docker run -it --rm k8s.gcr.io/kube-apiserver:v1.19.0 kube-
apiserver --help | grep enable-admission-plugins
```

...

```
    --enable-admission-plugins strings admission plugins
    that should be enabled in addition to default
    enabled ones (NamespaceLifecycle, LimitRanger,
```

```
ServiceAccount, TaintNodesByCondition, ...). Comma-
delimited list of admission plugins: AlwaysAdmit,
AlwaysDeny, AlwaysPullImages, CertificateApproval,
CertificateSigning, CertificateSubjectRestriction,
DefaultIngressClass, DefaultStorageClass, ...
```

Note   The output is concatenated as it is incredibly long, and we will not cover each admission plugin one by one. If you need further information about plugins, you can check the reference documentation.

In addition to the default admission controllers in kube-apiserver, adding new ones as webhooks during runtime is possible. Unlike the authentication and authorization plugins, it is possible to add or remove admission controllers when the cluster is running; therefore, they are called *dynamic admission controllers*.

Let's start with extending the authentication flow by developing webhooks and configuring the Kubernetes cluster.

Authentication Webhooks

Authentication webhooks extend the Kubernetes API flow by external security logic. Webhooks in Kubernetes are HTTP callbacks to the external systems. When a specific event happens in the cluster, the Kubernetes API server sends a structured request to the external service via HTTP POST. The webhook server is expected to return a structured response so that the Kubernetes API server continues operating. There are two essential parts to configure to run authentication webhooks: *Kubernetes API server* and *webhook server*. Let's start with the Kubernetes API server to let it know where to connect as a webhook.

Kubernetes API Server Configuration

Kubernetes API server runs in the control plane and needs to know where to connect as a webhook. The configuration is set via flags and configuration files of kube-apiserver binary. Therefore, the cluster admin, most probably you, should handle the setup. There are two fundamental flags for kube-apiserver for authentication webhook configuration:

- --authentication-token-webhook-config-file: A configuration file describing how to access the remote webhook service

- --authentication-token-webhook-cache-ttl: How long to cache authentication decisions with the default of two minutes

Note   There is also a version flag named as --authentication-token-webhook-version. It determines whether to use authentication.k8s.io/v1beta1 or authentication.k8s. io/v1 TokenReview objects to send/receive information from the webhook. The default is v1beta1 and used as it is in this chapter.

The authentication-token-webhook-config-file flag has no default value and needs a configuration file that is similar to kubeconfig.

Listing 3-2. Authentication token webhook config example

```
apiVersion: v1
kind: Config
clusters:
  - name: remote-auth-service
    cluster:
      certificate-authority: /path/to/ca.pem
      server: https://extend.k8s.io/authenticate
```

```
users:
  - name: remote-auth-service-user
    user:
      client-certificate: /path/to/cert.pem
      client-key: /path/to/key.pem
current-context: webhook
contexts:
- context:
    cluster: remote-auth-service
    user: remote-auth-service-user
  name: webhook
```

When the bearer token authentication is active, the Kubernetes API server connects to the server defined in the cluster and uses `certificate-authority` if necessary. In addition, the API server utilizes the `client-certificate` and `client-key` to communicate with the webhook server securely. Now, let's continue with the webhook server and the communication between Kubernetes API.

Webhook Server

When the API server is configured with a webhook token authentication, it will send a JSON request with the `TokenReview` object. A sample `TokenReview` object can be constructed as follows.

Listing 3-3. TokenReview object

```
{
  "apiVersion": "authentication.k8s.io/v1beta1",
  "kind": "TokenReview",
  "spec": {
    "token": "0x123...",
  }
}
```

The webhook server validates the incoming token and gathers user information. The remote server must fill the status field of the TokenReview object and send back the data. Successful validation of the bearer token would return the following TokenReview as an example.

Listing 3-4. TokenReview with a successful status

```
{
    "apiVersion": "authentication.k8s.io/v1beta1",
    "kind": "TokenReview",
    "status": {
        "authenticated": true,
        "user":{
            "username": "user@k8s.io",
            "uid": "21",
            "groups":[ "system", "qa" ]
        }
    }
}
```

Username, UID, and groups are the identifiers of the validated user. The information is essential for the authorization stage to decide who has access from which group. When the validation of the token fails, the webhook server should return a request similar to the following.

Listing 3-5. TokenReview with a failed status

```
{
    "apiVersion": "authentication.k8s.io/v1beta1",
    "kind": "TokenReview",
    "status": {
        "authenticated": false,
```

```
    "error": "Credentials are not validated"
  }
}
```

kube-apiserver uses the error message in TokenReview status when the webhook server rejects the user. It is possible to summarize the flow of TokenReview messages between the webhook and Kubernetes API server in Figure 3-2.

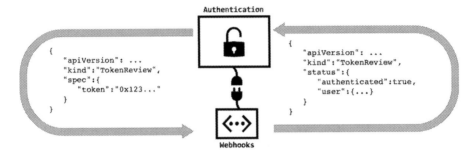

Figure 3-2. *Authentication message flow*

It is possible to have webhook servers internal or external to the Kubernetes clusters. In other words, you can run a server inside the Kubernetes cluster and use it as the webhook server. Kubernetes API server connects to the webhook server using HTTPS; therefore, you also need to set up TLS certificates. As an alternative, you can set your webhook server external to the cluster and make it available to the outside world. The critical point in both options is to have the webhook server up and running since authentication flow depends on it. In the following exercise, you will deploy a serverless webhook to Google Cloud and configure a local minikube cluster to use it as an authentication endpoint.

EXERCISE: SERVERLESS AUTHENTICATION WEBHOOK

The webhook server in this exercise will run on Google Cloud as a part of its serverless platform. You will start creating a cloud function and deploy it to Google Cloud. Then you will configure the local minikube cluster to use the address of the serverless function as an authentication webhook.

1. Open Google Cloud Console and head to *Compute* ➤ *Cloud Functions*. Click "**CREATE FUNCTION**" in the function listing view as in Figure 3-3.

Figure 3-3. *GCP Cloud Functions*

2. In the "Create function" view as shown in Figure 3-4, fill the name field and select "*Allow unauthenticated invocations*" and then click **NEXT**.

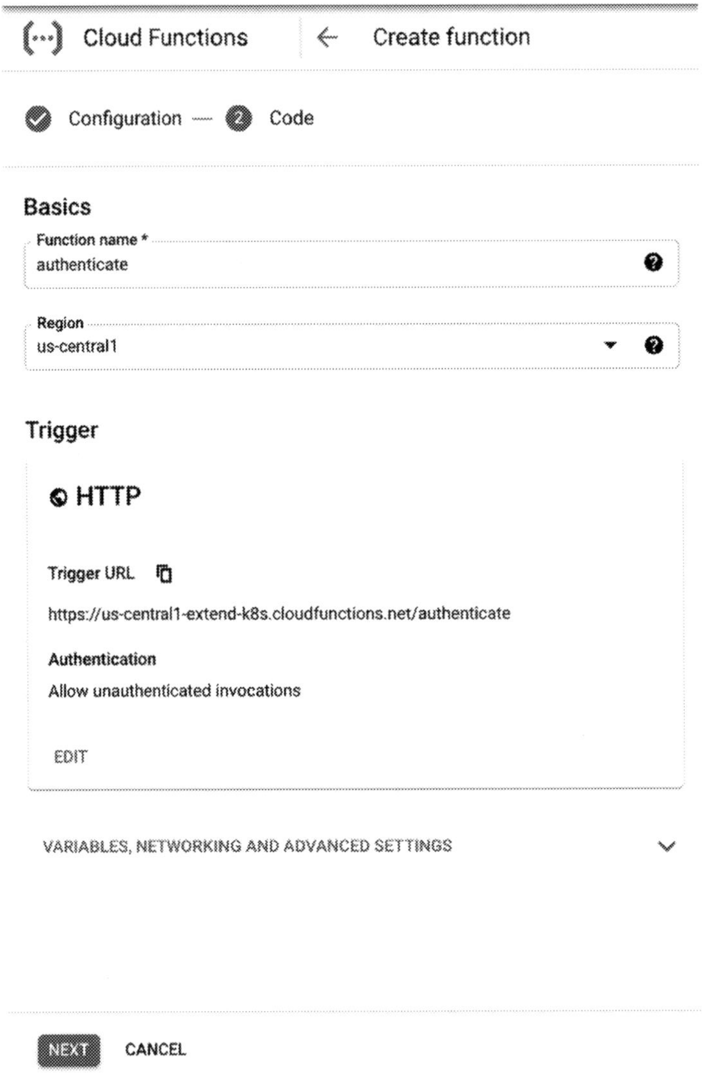

Figure 3-4. *Create function*

Note down the Trigger URL since you will use it in Step 5 as
SERVERLESS_ENDPOINT environment variable.

3. In the "Code" view, select **Go** as runtime and fill "Entry
    Point" field with **Authenticate**. Authenticate is the name of
    the function that Google Cloud will call when the serverless
    endpoint is reached. Change the contents of the function.go
    with the following content:

```go
package authenticate

import (
        "encoding/json"
        "errors"
        "log"
        "net/http"
        "strings"

        authentication "k8s.io/api/authentication/v1beta1"
)

func Authenticate(w http.ResponseWriter, r *http.Request) {
        decoder := json.NewDecoder(r.Body)
        var tr authentication.TokenReview
        err := decoder.Decode(&tr)
        if err != nil {
                handleError(w, err)
                return
        }

        user, err := logon(tr.Spec.Token)
        if err != nil {
                handleError(w, err)
                return
        }

        log.Printf("[Success] login as %s", user.username)
```

```go
        w.WriteHeader(http.StatusOK)
        trs := authentication.TokenReviewStatus{
                Authenticated: true,
                User: authentication.UserInfo{
                        Username: user.username,
                        Groups:   []string{user.group},
                },
        }
        tr.Status = trs
        json.NewEncoder(w).Encode(tr)
}

func handleError(w http.ResponseWriter, err error) {

        log.Println("[Error]", err.Error())

        tr := new(authentication.TokenReview)
        trs := authentication.TokenReviewStatus{
                Authenticated: false,
                Error: err.Error(),
        }
        tr.Status = trs

        w.WriteHeader(http.StatusUnauthorized)
        json.NewEncoder(w).Encode(tr)

}

func logon(token string) (*User, error) {
        data := strings.Split(token, ";")
        if len(data) < 3 {
                return nil, errors.New("no token data")
        }
```

```go
        for _, u := range allowed {
            if u.group == data[0] && u.username ==
            data[1] && u.password == data[2] {
                return &u, nil
            }
        }

        return nil, errors.New("no user found")
}

type User struct {
        username string
        password string
        group    string
}

var allowed = []User{
        {
                username: "minikube-user",
                group:    "system:masters",
                password: "mysecret",
        },
}
```

This file has the Authenticate HTTP endpoint to parse TokenReview data, log on the user, and send it back. It uses the logon helper function to search allowed users. There is only one permitted user: minikube-user with its valid token of system:masters;minikube-user;mysecret.

Change the contents of go.mod as follows:

```
module extend.k8s.io/authenticate

go 1.14

require k8s.io/api v0.19.0
```

In the `function.go`, we are using the Kubernetes Go client library; therefore, we list it as a requirement with `k8s.io/api`, version `v0.19.0`.

Click **DEPLOY** at the bottom of the page in Figure 3-5.

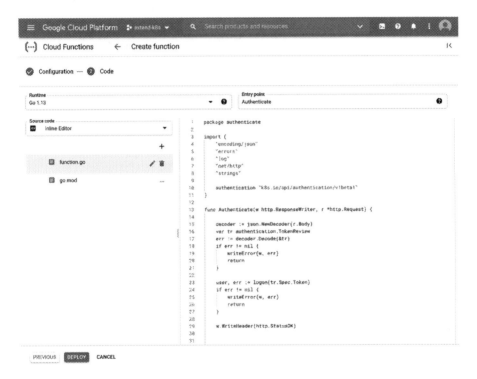

Figure 3-5. *Deployment of the function*

> **Note:** In order to build and deploy the function, you need to enable Cloud Build API in Cloud Console API Library view if you have not done before.

4. Wait in the function list view as in Figure 3-6 until there is a green check next to it.

Figure 3-6. *Successful deployment*

5. Create a local webhook config file `serverless-authn.yaml` with the following content:

```
apiVersion: v1
kind: Config
clusters:
  - name: serverless-authn
    cluster:
      server: SERVERLESS_ENDPOINT
users:
  - name: authn-user
current-context: webhook
contexts:
- context:
    cluster: serverless-authn
    user: authn-user
  name: webhook
```

Do not forget to change the SERVERLESS_ENDPOINT with the URL from Step 2.

6. Move the file to minikube files:

```
mkdir -p $HOME/.minikube/files/var/lib/minikube/certs
mv serverless-authn.yaml $HOME/.minikube/files/var/lib/
minikube/certs/serverless-authn.yaml
```

59

7. Start the minikube cluster with the extra flags:

```
$ minikube start --extra-config apiserver.authentication-
token-webhook-config-file=/var/lib/minikube/certs/
serverless-authn.yaml
☺  minikube v1.14.1 on Darwin 10.15.7
✦  Automatically selected the docker driver
👍  Starting control plane node minikube in cluster
   minikube
🔥  Creating docker container (CPUs=2, Memory=4000MB) ...
🐳  Preparing Kubernetes v1.19.2 on Docker 19.03.8 ...
    • apiserver.authentication-token-webhook-config-
    file=/var/lib/minikube/certs/serverless-authn.yaml
🔎  Verifying Kubernetes components...
🌟  Enabled addons: storage-provisioner, default-
   storageclass
🏄  Done! kubectl is now configured to use "minikube" by
   default
```

8. Create a new empty user and use it in the current context:

```
$ kubectl config set-credentials auth-test
User "auth-test" set.
$ kubectl config set-context --current --user=auth-test
Context "minikube" modified.
```

9. Run kubectl with the valid token and check the result:

```
$ kubectl get nodes --token="system:masters;minikube-
user;mysecret"
NAME        STATUS    ROLES    AGE     VERSION
minikube    Ready     master   116s    v1.19.2
```

As expected, Kubernetes API sends the output for listing the nodes.

10. Run `kubectl` with a random token and check the result:

```
$ kubectl get nodes --token="xyz"
error: You must be logged in to the server (Unauthorized)
```

11. Check for the serverless function logs in Google Cloud and see the webhook in action as shown in Figure 3-7.

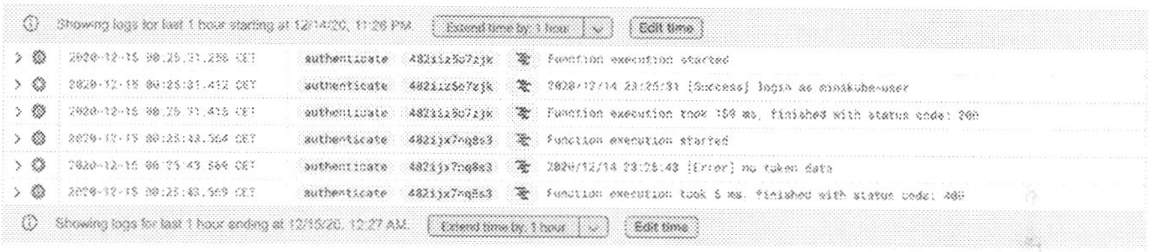

Figure 3-7. *Function logs*

The logs show the successful (first) and failed (second) logon activities.

In this exercise, you have exposed a public function and used it in your Kubernetes cluster. In your production setup, it is suggested to use a protected function instead.

In the following section, we will extend the Kubernetes API flow with custom authorization modules. We will learn the webhook and Kubernetes API server requirements and then implement custom decision logic to decide who can access or modify resources in the cluster.

Authorization Webhooks

Authorization webhooks extend the access control of Kubernetes API to implement custom policies. When a request passes the authentication stage, authorization modules evaluate the attributes in sequence. If any of the authorization modules approves or denies the request, the result is immediately returned. If the request is approved, the API request continues with the flow and moves to the next stages. Like the authentication stage, there are two basic configurations to run authorization webhooks in action: Kubernetes API server and webhook server.

Kubernetes API Server Configuration

kube-apiserver has flags to define authorization modes and webhook configuration. The authorization mode is set via --authorization-mode flag with the default value of AlwaysAllow. In other words, all authenticated requests are allowed in Kubernetes API by default. However, in the typical Kubernetes setup, the following authorization modes are enabled: RBAC and Node. Therefore, to add the webhook authorization, you need to update the flag value by adding Webhook. There are three essential flags to configure authorization webhook operations:

- --authorization-webhook-config-file: A configuration file to describe how to access and query the remote service. The flag is similar to the one in authentication, and it needs a configuration identical to kubeconfig. Ensure that the authorization webhook server address is correct and certificate data if necessary.

- --authorization-webhook-cache-authorized-ttl: Duration to cache the validated requests; the default is five minutes.

- --authorization-webhook-cache-unauthorized-ttl: Duration to cache the invalid requests; the default is 30 seconds.

> **Note**   There is also a version flag named as `--authorization-webhook-version`. It sets the API version of the `authorization.k8s.io` `SubjectAccessReview` to send to and expect from the webhook. The default is `v1beta1` and used as it is in the chapter.

Webhook Server

Kubernetes API server calls the webhook server by sending a `SubjectAccessReview` object to describe the action to be checked. The sent JSON object contains information about the resource, user, and request attributes. An example `SubjectAccessReview` to get pods in the namespace `default` by the user `ece` has the following structure.

Listing 3-6. SubjectAccessReview for pod listing

```
{
  "apiVersion": "authorization.k8s.io/v1beta1",
  "kind": "SubjectAccessReview",
  "spec": {
    "resourceAttributes": {
      "namespace": "default",
      "verb": "get",
      "group": "",
      "resource": "pods"
    },
    "user": "ece"
  }
}
```

When the non-resource paths in the Kubernetes API are called, such as /version or /metrics, the nonResourceAttributes field is sent to the webhook server. For instance, the Kubernetes API server will ship the following SubjectAccessReview when the user nursin calls the version endpoint.

Listing 3-7. SubjectAccessReview for version information

```
{
  "apiVersion": "authorization.k8s.io/v1beta1",
  "kind": "SubjectAccessReview",
  "spec": {
    "nonResourceAttributes": {
      "path": "/version",
      "verb": "get"
    },
    "user": "nursin"
  }
}
```

The webhook server responds to the SubjectAccessReview objects by filling their status fields. If the webhook server accepts the request, it could easily send the following data back to the Kubernetes API server.

Listing 3-8. Accepted response

```
{
  "apiVersion": "authorization.k8s.io/v1beta1",
  "kind": "SubjectAccessReview",
  "status": {
    "allowed": true
  }
}
```

On the other hand, there are two methods to deny a request in webhook servers. The first method only indicates that the request is not allowed as follows.

Listing 3-9. Rejected response

```
{
  "apiVersion": "authorization.k8s.io/v1beta1",
  "kind": "SubjectAccessReview",
  "status": {
    "allowed": false,
    "reason": "user has no access"
  }
}
```

When only the `allowed` field is set to false, other authorization modules are also checked if any one of them will allow it. If none of the authorization modules allow the request, it is denied by the API server. The second approach is to deny any request immediately and bypassing the remaining authorization modules. The response data is similar to the previous one with one simple addition.

Listing 3-10. Rejected and denied response

```
{
  "apiVersion": "authorization.k8s.io/v1beta1",
  "kind": "SubjectAccessReview",
  "status": {
    "allowed": false,
    "denied": true,
    "reason": "user has no access"
  }
}
```

The message flow between the Kubernetes API and authorization webhook servers can be summarized in Figure 3-8.

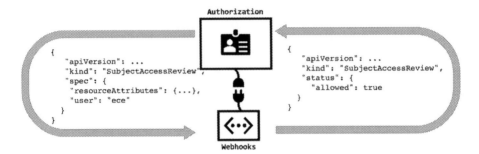

Figure 3-8. *Authorization message flow*

Although the message flow seems straightforward, the logic you will implement in the webhook server has no limits. You can design an authorization system to limit users from specific groups to take particular actions. Let's assume that you have two teams, *development* and *production*, and a *continuous deployment (CD)* system for releases. It is possible to create an authorization webhook to let the development team access *only reading pods*. Similarly, you can limit the production team to *update the deployments* and only allow the technical users from CD to *create new deployments*. Considering the team members are defined in any other external system such as LDAP or GitHub, the webhook server will have the involved logic and extend Kubernetes authorization.

In the following exercise, you will create a serverless authorization webhook to make a namespace in Kubernetes read-only. The users will only read, list, or watch resources but cannot update, create, or delete in the protected namespace.

EXERCISE: AUTHORIZATION WEBHOOK FOR READ-ONLY NAMESPACE

In this exercise, you will develop a serverless webhook in Google Cloud Functions. The webhook will give authorization decisions to make the namespace protected read-only. Then, you will start a local minikube cluster and configure it to use the serverless endpoint as an authorization webhook.

1. Open Google Cloud Console and click *Compute* ➤ *Cloud Functions* in the main menu. Click "CREATE FUNCTION" in the function listing view in Figure 3-9.

Figure 3-9. *GCP Cloud Functions*

2. In the "Create function" view in Figure 3-10, fill the name field and select "Allow unauthenticated invocations" and then click NEXT.

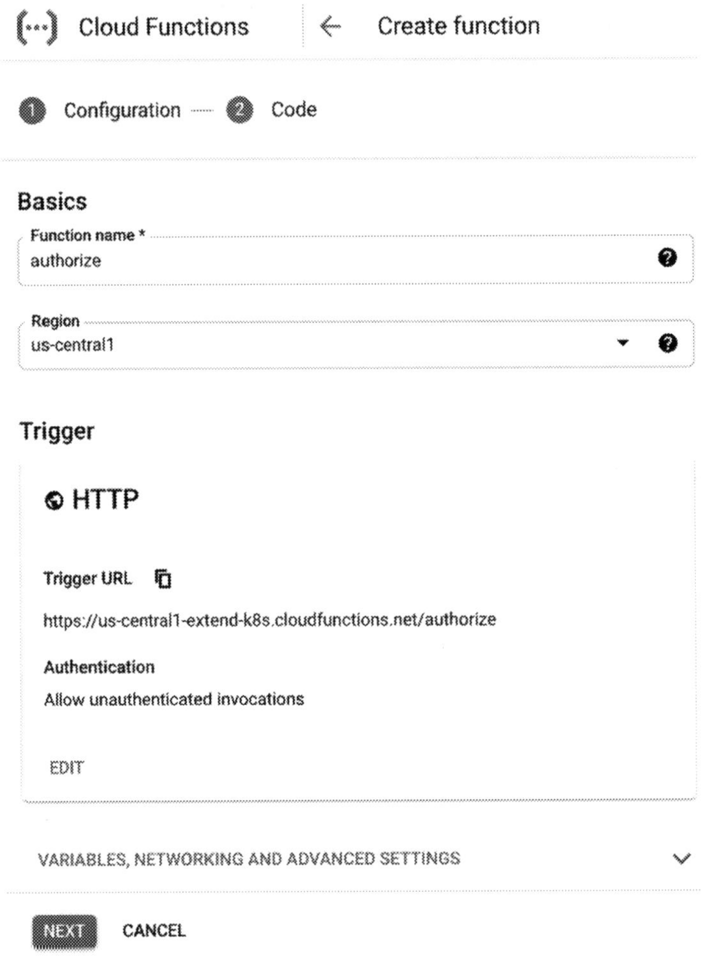

(···) Cloud Functions   ←   Create function

① Configuration ···· ② Code

Basics

Function name *
authorize   ❓

Region
us-central1   ▾ ❓

Trigger

◉ HTTP

Trigger URL   ⎘

https://us-central1-extend-k8s.cloudfunctions.net/authorize

Authentication
Allow unauthenticated invocations

EDIT

VARIABLES, NETWORKING AND ADVANCED SETTINGS   ⌄

[NEXT]   CANCEL

Figure 3-10. *Create function*

In the "Code" view, select Go as runtime and fill "Entry Point" field
with `Authorize`. It is the function in our deployment to be called by
when the serverless endpoint is reached. Change the contents of the
`function.go` with the following content:

```
package authorize
```

```go
import (
        "encoding/json"
        "fmt"
        "log"
        "net/http"

        authorization "k8s.io/api/authorization/v1beta1"
)

const NAMESPACE = "protected"

func Authorize(w http.ResponseWriter, r *http.Request) {

        decoder := json.NewDecoder(r.Body)
        var sar authorization.SubjectAccessReview
        err := decoder.Decode(&sar)
        if err != nil {
                log.Println("[Error]", err.Error())

                sar := new(authorization.SubjectAccessReview)
                status := authorization.
                SubjectAccessReviewStatus{
                        Allowed: false,
                        Reason:  err.Error(),
                }
                sar.Status = status

                w.WriteHeader(http.StatusUnauthorized)
                json.NewEncoder(w).Encode(sar)
                return
        }

        if sar.Spec.ResourceAttributes != nil {
                v := sar.Spec.ResourceAttributes.Verb
                n := sar.Spec.ResourceAttributes.Namespace
```

```
            if n == NAMESPACE && (v == "create" || v ==
            "delete" || v == "update") {

                    log.Printf("[Not Allowed] %s
                    in namespace %s", sar.Spec.
                    ResourceAttributes.Verb, NAMESPACE)

                    response := new(authorization.
                    SubjectAccessReview)
                    status := authorization.
                    SubjectAccessReviewStatus{
                            Allowed: false,
                            Denied:  true,
                            Reason:  fmt.Sprintf("%s is not
                            allowed in the namespace: %s",
                            sar.Spec.ResourceAttributes.Verb,
                            NAMESPACE),
                    }
                    response.Status = status
                    json.NewEncoder(w).Encode(response)
                    return

            }
    }

    response := new(authorization.SubjectAccessReview)
    status := authorization.SubjectAccessReviewStatus{
            Allowed: true,
    }
    response.Status = status
    json.NewEncoder(w).Encode(response)
}
```

In this file, there is only one function named Authorize. It is an
HTTP handler to parse the incoming SubjectAccessReview data.
If the incoming data has ResourceAttributes, it checks whether

the namespace is `protected` and verbs are `create`, `delete`, or `update`. When such a request is found, it rejects by sending `Allowed: false` and `Denied: true`. For all other requests, it allows the request and lets other authorization modules decide. Change the contents of `go.mod` as follows:

```
module extend.k8s.io/authorize

go 1.13

require k8s.io/api v0.19.0
```

In the `function.go`, we are using the Kubernetes Go client library; therefore, we list it as a dependency with `k8s.io/api`, version `v0.19.0`.

Click *DEPLOY* at the bottom of the page in Figure 3-11.

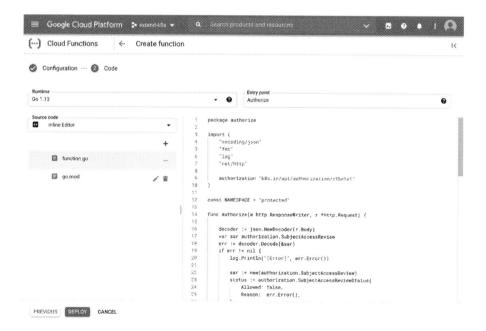

Figure 3-11. *Deployment of the function*

3. Wait in the function list view in Figure 3-12 until there is a green check next to it.

Figure 3-12. *Successful deployment*

Create a local webhook config file `serverless-authz.yaml` with the following content:

```
apiVersion: v1
kind: Config
clusters:
  - name: serverless-authz
    cluster:
      server: SERVERLESS_ENDPOINT
users:
  - name: authz-user
current-context: webhook
contexts:
- context:
    cluster: serverless-authz
    user: authz-user
  name: webhook
```

Do not forget to change the `SERVERLESS_ENDPOINT` with the URL from Step 2.

4. Move the file to minikube files:

```
$ mkdir -p $HOME/.minikube/files/var/lib/minikube/certs
$ mv serverless-authz.yaml $HOME/.minikube/files/var/lib/
minikube/certs/serverless-authz.yaml
```

5. Start the minikube cluster with the extra flags:

```
$ minikube start \
--extra-config apiserver.authorization-
mode=Node,RBAC,Webhook \
--extra-config apiserver.authorization-webhook-config-
file=/var/lib/minikube/certs/serverless-authz.yaml
```

😄 minikube v1.14.1 on Darwin 10.15.7
✦ Automatically selected the docker driver
👍 Starting control plane node minikube in cluster
    minikube
🐳 Creating docker container (CPUs=2, Memory=4000MB) ...
🎱 Preparing Kubernetes v1.19.2 on Docker 19.03.8 ...
    ▪ apiserver.authorization-mode=Node,RBAC,Webhook
    ▪ apiserver.authorization-webhook-config-file=/var/
      lib/minikube/certs/serverless-authz.yaml
🔎 Verifying Kubernetes components...
🌟 Enabled addons: storage-provisioner, default-
    storageclass
🏄 Done! kubectl is now configured to use "minikube" by
    default

This command starts a local minikube cluster with two extra
config parameters. The first config adds webhook to the
authorization modes, and the second one indicates the location
of the config file from Step 3.

6. Check what the user is allowed to do with the following commands:

```
$ kubectl auth can-i create deployments --as developer
yes
```

It shows that it is possible to create deployments in the default namespace.

```
$ kubectl auth can-i create deployments --as developer
--namespace protected

no - create is not allowed the namespace protected

$ kubectl auth can-i delete secrets --as developer
--namespace protected

no - delete is not allowed in the namespace protected
```

However, it is not allowed to create deployments or delete secrets in the protected namespace. It ensures that the resources in the namespace stay as it is in a read-only mode.

```
$ kubectl auth can-i list pods --as developer --namespace
protected
yes
```

On the other hand, it is possible to list the pods in the protected namespace which is what we wanted in a read-only mode.

7. Check for the serverless function logs in Google Cloud and see the webhook in action as in Figure 3-13.

```
▶ ▓ 2020-12-16T12:09:48.512690877Z  authorize  900bulpwj4d7   Function execution started
▶ ░ 2020-12-16T12:09:48.52??  authorize  900bulpwj4d7   2020/12/16 12:09:48 [Not Allowed] create in namespace protected
▶ ▓ 2020-12-16T12:09:48.528S225042  authorize  900bulpwj4d7   Function execution took 16 ms, finished with status code: 200
▶ ▓ 2020-12-16T12:11:05.63617643BZ  authorize  900btkcugdjc   Function execution started
▶ ▓ 2020-12-16T12:11:05.654120407Z  authorize  900btkcugdjc   Function execution took 19 ms, finished with status code: 200
▶ ▓ 2020-12-16T12:11:27.402816002  authorize  900bqxl1Srcz   Function execution started
▶ ░ 2020-12-16T12:11:27.404Z  authorize  900bqxl1Srcz   2020/12/16 12:11:27 [Not Allowed] delete in namespace protected
▶ ▓ 2020-12-16T12:11:27.409100351Z  authorize  900bqxl1Srcz   Function execution took 3 ms, finished with status code: 200
```

Figure 3-13. *Function logs*

The logs indicate the creation and the deletion requests are not allowed by the authorization webhook.

In the following section, we will extend the Kubernetes API flow with its last stage: admission controllers. Admission controllers are the last steps to check or mutate the requests before persisting into the etcd storage. We will learn the admission webhook setup and how to define dynamically to extend and implement custom requirements.

Dynamic Admission Controllers

Admission controllers are the last stage in Kubernetes API flow just before the persistence of the objects. These controllers intercept the requests to validate or mutate the resources. There are already various admission controllers packaged into kube-apiserver binary with the addition of two extension points: MutatingAdmissionWebhook and ValidatingAdmissionWebhook. These extension points execute mutating and validating admission control webhooks, which are dynamically defined in Kubernetes API. Unlike the authentication and authorization webhooks, you could create, update, or delete admission controllers while the cluster is up and running. Therefore, they are mostly covered under the section "Dynamic Admission Controllers."

Admission webhooks are essential for the Kubernetes control plane and its operation. Mutating admission webhooks enable setting complex default values or injecting fields, whereas validating webhooks are critical for controlling what is deployed into the cluster. Firstly, mutating webhooks are called in serial since each one can modify the resource objects. Then, all validating webhooks are called in parallel; if any of them rejects the request, it is denied by the API server.

There are two aspects to configure and set up to extend the admission control mechanism: webhook configuration resources and webhook server. Let's first focus on webhook configuration resources to let Kubernetes API know where and when to call webhooks.

Webhook Configuration Resources

Dynamic configuration of the admission controllers is handled by `ValidatingWebhookConfiguration` and `MutatingWebhookConfiguration` API resources. An example of a validating webhook can be defined for pod creation as follows.

Listing 3-11. Webhook configuration example

```
apiVersion: admissionregistration.k8s.io/v1
kind: ValidatingWebhookConfiguration
metadata:
  name: "validation.extend-k8s.io"
webhooks:
- name: "validation.extend-k8s.io"
  rules:
  - apiGroups:    [""]
    apiVersions: ["v1"]
    operations:   ["CREATE"]
    resources:    ["pods"]
```

```
  scope:        "Namespaced"
clientConfig:
  url: "https://extend-k8s.io/validate"
admissionReviewVersions: ["v1", "v1beta1"]
sideEffects: None
```

There are two crucial parts of the API resource: `rules` and `clientConfig`. When the Kubernetes API server receives a request that matches the rules, an HTTP request is made to the webhook defined in `clientConfig`. For instance, with the definition in Listing 3-11, the API server will call `https://extend-k8s.io/validate` when a new pod is created.

Mutating webhook configuration is done with the `MutatingWebhookConfiguration` resources with a similar structure. An example webhook to call when secrets are created can be defined as follows.

Listing 3-12. Webhook configuration example

```
apiVersion: admissionregistration.k8s.io/v1
kind: MutatingWebhookConfiguration
metadata:
  name: "mutation.extend-k8s.io"
webhooks:
- name: "mutation.extend-k8s.io"
  rules:
  - apiGroups:    [""]
    apiVersions:  ["v1"]
    operations:   ["CREATE"]
    resources:    ["secrets"]
    scope:        "Namespaced"
```

```
clientConfig:
  service:
    namespace: "extension"
    name: "mutation-service"
  caBundle: "CiOtLSOtQk...tLSOK"
admissionReviewVersions: ["v1", "v1beta1"]
sideEffects: None
```

When a secret creation request is received, the Kubernetes API server will reach the 443 port of the mutation-service running in the extension namespace. It will use the caBundle to validate the TLS certificates of the webhook server. In the following section, we will cover the message flow between admission controller webhooks.

Webhook Server

Kubernetes API server sends a POST request with AdmissionReview object to define the request and its attributes. For example, the webhook server will receive an item similar to the following when a new pod is created.

Listing 3-13. AdmissionReview example

```
{
  "apiVersion": "admission.k8s.io/v1",
  "kind": "AdmissionReview",
  "request": {

    "uid": "4b8bd269-bfc7-4dd5-8022-7ca57a334fa3",

    "name": "example-app",
    "namespace": "default",

    "operation": "CREATE",
```

```
  "kind": {"group":"","version":"v1","kind":"Pod"},
  "requestKind":  {"group":"","version":"v1","kind":"Pod"},

  "resource": {"group":"","version":"v1","resource":"pods"},
  "requestResource": {"group":"","version":"v1","resource":
  "pods"},

  "object": {"apiVersion":"v1","kind":"Pod",...},

  "userInfo": {
    "username": "minikube",
    "groups": ["system:authenticated"]
  },

  "options": {"apiVersion":"meta.k8s.io/v1","kind":
  "CreateOptions",...},
  "dryRun": false
  }
}
```

The admission review object is reasonably packed since it transmits all the information related to the request and the related item. For instance, in Listing 3-13 there is a complete pod definition in the `request.object` field. Webhook server is required to send an `AdmissionReview` object again with the response field loaded. A minimal acceptance response can be constructed as follows.

Listing 3-14. Accepted admission review response

```
{
  "apiVersion": "admission.k8s.io/v1",
  "kind": "AdmissionReview",
```

```
"response": {
  "uid": "<value from request.uid>",
  "allowed": true
}
}
```

Similarly, a simple rejection can be sent with the following data.

Listing 3-15. Rejected admission review response

```
{
  "apiVersion": "admission.k8s.io/v1",
  "kind": "AdmissionReview",
  "response": {
    "uid": "<value from request.uid>",
    "allowed": false
  }
}
```

Mutating webhooks are also expected to modify the objects in the requests. Therefore, the webhook server should send the changes in the AdmissionReview response. Kubernetes supports JSONPatch kind of operations to change fields of resources. For instance, a JSONPatch to change the replicas to 5 of a deployment can be constructed as follows: [{"op": "replace", "path": "/spec/replicas", "value": 5}]. When the patch is transported inside AdmissionReview, it will be encoded using base64 as follows.

Listing 3-16. Accepted admission review response with patch

```
{
  "apiVersion": "admission.k8s.io/v1",
  "kind": "AdmissionReview",
```

```
  "response": {
    "uid": "<value from request.uid>",
    "allowed": true,
    "patchType": "JSONPatch",
    "patch": "W3sib3AiOiAicmVwbGFjZSIsICJwYXRoIjogIi9zcGVjL3J
    lcGxpY2FzIiwgInZhbHVlIjogNX1d"
  }
}
```

When the Kubernetes API gets the response with a patch, it will apply the changes on the resource and continue processing with the next admission controllers. The summary of the messages between the webhook server and Kubernetes API can be summarized in Figure 3-14.

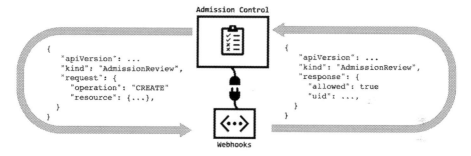

Figure 3-14. *Admission webhook message flow*

Both mutating and validating webhooks are critical components in the API flow since they can programmatically change the resources and accept or reject the requests. It could create chaos quickly when used with negligence or inadequate design. There are three best practices to follow for a reliable admission control setup:

- **Idempotence**: Mutating webhooks should be idempotent; in other words, the admission webhook can be called multiple times without changing the result after the first run.

- **Availability**: Admission webhooks are called as part of Kubernetes API operations. Therefore, they should evaluate and return the responses as quickly as possible, like all other webhook servers, to minimize the total latency.

- **Deadlocks**: If the webhook endpoints are running inside the cluster, they can interfere with its resources such as pods, secrets, or volumes. Therefore, it is recommended not to run admission controllers on the namespace of the webhook.

In the following exercises, you will first create a dynamic validation admission webhook to check and verify the container images. In the second exercise, you will inject environment variables to the pods running in specific namespaces with mutating admission webhooks.

EXERCISE: VALIDATING WEBHOOK FOR CONTAINER IMAGE CHECK

In this exercise, you will develop a serverless webhook in Google Cloud Functions. The webhook will validate pod creation requests by evaluating the container images. It will only allow container images with the nginx and reject all other pods. You will then start a GKE cluster and configure a namespace of the cluster to use the validating webhook.

1. Open Google Cloud Console and click Activate Cloud Shell in the navigation bar. It should load a terminal in your browser to run commands like in Figure 3-15.

Figure 3-15. *GCP Cloud Shell*

2. Create a folder named `validation` and change the directory
    into it:

```
$ mkdir validation
$ cd validation
```

Create a file named `function.go` in the terminal or open the
editor inside Google Cloud Console. The file should have the
following content:

```go
package validate

import (
        "encoding/json"
        "log"
        "net/http"
        "regexp"

        admission "k8s.io/api/admission/v1"
        corev1 "k8s.io/api/core/v1"
        metav1 "k8s.io/apimachinery/pkg/apis/meta/v1"
)

func Validation(w http.ResponseWriter, r *http.Request) {

        ar := new(admission.AdmissionReview)
        err := json.NewDecoder(r.Body).Decode(ar)
        if err != nil {
                handleError(w, nil, err)
                return
        }

        response := &admission.AdmissionResponse{
                UID:     ar.Request.UID,
                Allowed: true,
        }
```

```go
        pod := &corev1.Pod{}
        if err := json.Unmarshal(ar.Request.Object.Raw,
        pod); err != nil {
                handleError(w, ar, err)
                return
        }

        re := regexp.MustCompile(`(?m)(nginx|nginx:\S+)`)

        for _, c := range pod.Spec.Containers {

                if !re.MatchString(c.Image) {
                        response.Allowed = false
                        break
                }
        }

        responseAR := &admission.AdmissionReview{
                TypeMeta: metav1.TypeMeta{
                        Kind:       "AdmissionReview",
                        APIVersion: "admission.k8s.io/v1",
                },
                Response: response,
        }

        json.NewEncoder(w).Encode(responseAR)
}

func handleError(w http.ResponseWriter, ar *admission.
AdmissionReview, err error) {

        if err != nil {
                log.Println("[Error]", err.Error())
        }
```

```
response := &admission.AdmissionResponse{
    Allowed: false,
}
if ar != nil {
    response.UID = ar.Request.UID
}

ar.Response = response
json.NewEncoder(w).Encode(ar)
}
```

The file has an HTTP handler named Validation to parse incoming AdmissionReview objects and check the images of all containers. When it finds a container image not fitting to nginx, it will directly reject the review and send the response. Otherwise, it will accept by sending Allowed: true.

Create another file named go.mod with the following content:

```
module extend.k8s.io/validate

go 1.13

require (
  k8s.io/api v0.19.0
  k8s.io/apimachinery v0.19.0
)
```

In the function.go, we are using the Kubernetes Go client library; therefore, we list it as a dependency with k8s.io/api and k8s.io/apimachinery,version v0.19.0.

3. Deploy the function with the following command:

```
$ gcloud functions deploy validate --allow-
unauthenticated --entry-point=Validation --trigger-http
--runtime=go113
```

```
..
entryPoint: Validation
httpsTrigger:
  url: https://us-central1-extend-k8s.cloudfunctions.net/
  validate
...
runtime: go113
...
status: ACTIVE
timeout: 60s
..
versionId: '1'
```

Copy the `httpsTrigger` URL to use in the following steps.

4. Create a Kubernetes cluster with the following command:

```
$ gcloud container clusters create test-
validation --num-nodes=1 --region=us-central1

Creating cluster test-validation in us-central1...
Cluster is being health-checked (master is healthy)...
done.
kubeconfig entry generated for test-validation.

NAME             LOCATION      MASTER_VERSION
MASTER_IP       MACHINE_TYPE   NODE_VERSION
NUM_NODES  STATUS
test-validation  us-central1  1.16.15-gke.4300
34.69.30.171  n1-standard-1  1.16.15-gke.4300
3          RUNNING
```

Note   In order to create a Kubernetes cluster, you need to enable Kubernetes Engine API in Cloud Console API Library view if you have not done before.

5. Create a namespace and label it:

```
$ kubectl create namespace nginx-only
namespace/nginx-only created
$ kubectl label namespace nginx-only nginx=true
namespace/nginx-only labeled
```

6. Create a file with the name validating-webhook.yaml with the following content:

```
apiVersion: admissionregistration.k8s.io/v1
kind: ValidatingWebhookConfiguration
metadata:
  name: nginx.validate.extend.k8s
webhooks:
- name: nginx.validate.extend.k8s
  namespaceSelector:
      matchLabels:
        nginx: "true"
  rules:
  - apiGroups:    [""]
    apiVersions: ["v1"]
    operations:  ["CREATE"]
    resources:   ["pods"]
    scope:        "Namespaced"
  clientConfig:
    url: https://us-central1-extend-k8s.cloudfunctions.
    net/validate
  admissionReviewVersions: ["v1", "v1beta1"]
  sideEffects: None
  timeoutSeconds: 10
```

The file will create a validating webhook to be called when a new pod is created in the namespaces labeled with nginx=true. Do not forget to change the url to the one copied in Step 3.

Deploy the validating webhook conifguration with the following code:

```
$ kubectl apply -f validating-webhook.yaml
validatingwebhookconfiguration.admissionregistration.k8s.
io/nginx.validate.extend.k8s created
```

7. Create pod with `nginx` image in the `nginx-only` namespace:

```
$ kubectl run --generator=run-pod/v1 nginx --image=nginx
--namespace=nginx-only
pod/nginx created
```

The pod is created since the admission webhook allows only running `nginx` images.

8. Create a pod with `busybox` image in the `nginx-only` namespace:

```
$ kubectl run --generator=run-pod/v1 busybox
--image=busybox --namespace=nginx-only
Error from server: admission webhook "nginx.validate.
extend.k8s" denied the request without explanation
```

Admission webhook denied the image name `busybox` in the specified namespace. It shows that both the webhook server and Kubernetes API server are configured correctly to extend validating admission controllers.

9. Delete the cloud function and Kubernetes cluster to avoid extra cloud expenses:

```
$ gcloud container clusters delete test-validation
--region=us-central1
The following clusters will be deleted.
 - [test-validation] in [us-central1]
Do you want to continue (Y/n)?  Y
Deleting cluster test-validation...done.
```

```
$ gcloud functions delete validate
Resource
[projects/extend-k8s/locations/us-central1/functions/
validate] will be deleted.
Do you want to continue (Y/n)?  Y
Waiting for operation to finish...done.
Deleted
```

EXERCISE: MUTATING WEBHOOK FOR ENVIRONMENT VARIABLE INJECTION

In this exercise, you will develop a serverless webhook in Google Cloud Functions. The webhook will mutate the incoming request while creating new pods. It will inject an environment variable DEBUG with the value true for the pods created in the namespace labeled as debug=true. In addition, you will start and configure a GKE cluster to see the webhook in action.

1. Open Google Cloud Console and click Activate Cloud Shell in the navigation bar. It should load a terminal in your browser to run commands like in Figure 3-16.

Figure 3-16. *GCP Cloud Shell*

2. Create a folder named mutation and change the directory into it:

```
$ mkdir mutation
$ cd mutation
```

Create a file named `function.go` in the terminal with the following content:

```go
package mutator

import (
        "encoding/json"
        "log"
        "net/http"

        admission "k8s.io/api/admission/v1"
        corev1 "k8s.io/api/core/v1"
        metav1 "k8s.io/apimachinery/pkg/apis/meta/v1"
)

func Mutation(w http.ResponseWriter, r *http.Request) {

        ar := new(admission.AdmissionReview)
        err := json.NewDecoder(r.Body).Decode(ar)
        if err != nil {
                handleError(w, nil, err)
                return
        }
        pod := &corev1.Pod{}
        if err := json.Unmarshal(ar.Request.Object.Raw,
        pod); err != nil {
                handleError(w, ar, err)
                return
        }

        for i := 0; i < len(pod.Spec.Containers); i++ {
                pod.Spec.Containers[i].Env = append(pod.Spec.
                Containers[i].Env, corev1.EnvVar{
                        Name:  "DEBUG",
                        Value: "true",
                })
        }
```

```go
containersBytes, err := json.Marshal(&pod.Spec.
Containers)
if err != nil {
      handleError(w, ar, err)
      return
}

patch := []JSONPatchEntry{
      {
            OP:    "replace",
            Path:  "/spec/containers",
            Value: containersBytes,
      },
}

patchBytes, err := json.Marshal(&patch)
if err != nil {
      handleError(w, ar, err)
      return

}

patchType := admission.PatchTypeJSONPatch

response := &admission.AdmissionResponse{
      UID:       ar.Request.UID,
      Allowed:   true,
      Patch:     patchBytes,
      PatchType: &patchType,
}

responseAR := &admission.AdmissionReview{
      TypeMeta: metav1.TypeMeta{
            Kind:       "AdmissionReview",
            APIVersion: "admission.k8s.io/v1",
      },
```

```
            Response: response,
    }

    json.NewEncoder(w).Encode(responseAR)
}

type JSONPatchEntry struct {
    OP    string           `json:"op"`
    Path  string           `json:"path"`
    Value json.RawMessage `json:"value,omitempty"`
}

func handleError(w http.ResponseWriter, ar *admission.
AdmissionReview, err error) {

    if err != nil {
        log.Println("[Error]", err.Error())
    }

    response := &admission.AdmissionResponse{
        Allowed: false,
    }
    if ar != nil {
        response.UID = ar.Request.UID
    }

    ar.Response = response
    json.NewEncoder(w).Encode(ar)
}
```

The function has an HTTP handler named `Mutation` to parse `AdmissionReview` and prepare a response. It first adds environment variables to all containers in the pods and then creates a `JSONPatch`. Finally, it sends an approved `AdmissionReview` response with patch data.

Create another file named go.mod with the following content:

```
module extend.k8s.io/mutate

go 1.13

require (
  k8s.io/api v0.19.0
  k8s.io/apimachinery v0.19.0
)
```

In the function.go, we are using the Kubernetes Go client library; therefore, we list it as a dependency with k8s.io/api and k8s.io/apimachinery, version v0.19.0.

3. Deploy the function with the following command:

```
$ gcloud functions deploy mutate --allow-unauthenticated
--entry-point=Mutation --trigger-http --runtime=go113
..
entryPoint: Mutation
httpsTrigger:
  url: https://us-central1-extend-k8s.cloudfunctions.net/
  mutate
...
runtime: go113
...
status: ACTIVE
timeout: 60s
..
versionId: '1'
```

Copy the httpsTrigger URL to use in Step 6.

4. Create a Kubernetes cluster with the following command:

```
$ gcloud container clusters create test-mutation --num-
nodes=1 --region=us-central1

Creating cluster test-mutation in us-central1...
Cluster is being health-checked (master is healthy)...
done.
kubeconfig entry generated for test-mutation.

NAME                LOCATION       MASTER_VERSION
MASTER_IP       MACHINE_TYPE   NODE_VERSION
NUM_NODES   STATUS
test-mutation   us-central1   1.16.15-gke.4300
34.122.242.6   n1-standard-1   1.16.15-gke.4300
3               RUNNING
```

5. Create a namespace and label it:

```
$ kubectl create namespace testing
namespace/testing created
$ kubectl label namespace testing debug=true
namespace/testing labeled
```

6. Create a file with the name mutating-webhook.yaml with the following content. Do not forget to change the <httpsTrigger> with the URL from Step 3:

```
apiVersion: admissionregistration.k8s.io/v1
kind: MutatingWebhookConfiguration
metadata:
  name: debug.mutate.extend.k8s
webhooks:
- name: debug.mutate.extend.k8s
  namespaceSelector:
    matchLabels:
      debug: "true"
```

```
rules:
- apiGroups:    [""]
  apiVersions: ["v1"]
  operations:  ["CREATE"]
  resources:   ["pods"]
  scope:        "Namespaced"
clientConfig:
  url: <httpsTrigger>
admissionReviewVersions: ["v1", "v1beta1"]
sideEffects: None
timeoutSeconds: 10
```

The file will create a mutating webhook to be called when
a new pod is created in the namespaces labeled with
debug=true.

Deploy the mutating webhook configuration with the following code:

```
$ kubectl apply -f mutating-webhook.yaml
mutatingwebhookconfiguration.admissionregistration.k8s.
io/debug.mutate.extend.k8s created
```

7. Create pod in testing namespace:

```
$ kubectl run --generator=run-pod/v1 nginx --image=nginx
--namespace testing
pod/nginx created
```

Check for the environment variables in the nginx pod:

```
$ kubectl --namespace testing exec nginx -- env | grep
DEBUG
DEBUG=true
```

The pod has DEBUG=true environment variable, which is
injected by the mutating webhook. It shows that both the

webhook server and Kubernetes API server are configured
correctly to extend mutating admission controllers.

8. Create pod in default namespace:

```
$ kubectl run --generator=run-pod/v1 nginx --image=nginx
```

```
pod/nginx created
```

Check for the environment variables in the nginx pod:

```
$ kubectl exec nginx -- env | grep DEBUG
```

As expected, there are no environment variables found in the
pods living in the default namespace.

9. Delete the cloud function and Kubernetes cluster to avoid extra
cloud expenses:

```
$ gcloud container clusters delete test-mutation
--region=us-central1
The following clusters will be deleted.
 - [test-mutation] in [us-central1]
Do you want to continue (Y/n)?  Y
Deleting cluster test-mutation...done.
$ gcloud functions delete mutate
Resource
[projects/extend-k8s/locations/us-central1/functions/
mutate] will be deleted.
Do you want to continue (Y/n)?  Y
Waiting for operation to finish...done.
Deleted
```

Key Takeaways

- Every request to Kubernetes API goes through the authentication, authorization, and admission control stages in Kubernetes API flow.

- Webhooks can extend each stage in the Kubernetes API flow.

- Authentication webhooks enable validating bearer tokens with custom logic and external systems.

- Authorization webhooks enable verifying the user and control who can access which resources in the cluster.

- Dynamic admission controllers can modify related resources and validate the incoming API requests.

In the following chapter, we will extend the Kubernetes API with custom resources and the custom resources' automation, namely, operators.

CHAPTER 4

Extending the Kubernetes API

When I look at the human brain I'm still in awe of it.

—Benjamin "Ben" Solomon Carson
Neurosurgeon, American
politician, and author

Kubernetes API is the brain of the cloud-native container management system; it makes you feel admiration, respect, and amazement at the same time. It is a complex API with multiple layers, various resources, and, fortunately, two extension points. This chapter will focus on extending the Kubernetes API by creating custom resources and API aggregation. At the end of this chapter, you will be able to create custom resources and controllers; namely, you will implement a Kubernetes operator. In addition, you will create and deploy extension API servers and use aggregated APIs in action.

Let's start with an overview of Kubernetes API and its extension points.

© Onur Yilmaz 2021
O. Yilmaz, *Extending Kubernetes*, https://doi.org/10.1007/978-1-4842-7095-0_4

Kubernetes API Overview

Kubernetes API is the core foundation of the system. All internal and external operations to the cluster are *requests* to the API server. Consequently, everything in Kubernetes is an *API object* with its corresponding actions. The official versioned reference document has all the API objects with extensive information and examples, such as the v1.19 reference.

The API is a resource-based interface to read, create, update, or delete resources. The `kube-apiserver` component serves the API with its HTTP REST endpoints. Thus, every action by the control plane, node, or end users is a form of HTTP call to the `kube-apiserver`. Let's assume you want to create a new pod. `kubectl create` command sends a request to the Kubernetes API server with the payload of pod definition. The request is an HTTP POST to the `/api/v1/namespaces/{namespace}/pods` endpoint as mentioned in the reference in Figure 4-1.

Create

create a Pod

HTTP Request

POST /api/v1/namespaces/{namespace}/pods

Path Parameters

Parameter	Description
namespace	object name and auth scope, such as for teams and projects

Body Parameters

Parameter	Description
body Pod	

Response

Code	Description
200 Pod	OK
201 Pod	Created
202 Pod	Accepted

Figure 4-1. *Pod creation reference*

Then, kube-scheduler schedules the pod to a node. As expected, the scheduling is not an imperative command but a declarative Kubernetes resource: Binding. You can create a Binding request with node and pod as follows.

101

Listing 4-1. Example Binding

```
apiVersion: v1
kind: Binding
metadata:
  name: pod-to-be-assigned
  namespace: default
target:
  apiVersion: v1
  kind: Node
  name: available-node
```

kube-scheduler sends Binding resources to /api/v1/namespaces/
{namespace}/bindings endpoint via an HTTP POST request. Then
kubelet does its magic on the node to create containers, attach volumes,
and wait for its readiness. During that time, kubelet updates the status of
the pod, which is a subresource in Kubernetes. The status endpoint is
/api/v1/namespaces/{namespace}/pods/{name}/status, and updates are
sent via PATCH requests. Finally, you list the pods in your local workstation
using the kubectl get pods command. Let's debug the command with
some logs to check for its HTTP requests.

Listing 4-2. Getting pods with additional logs

```
$ kubectl get pods -v 9
...
* Starting client certificate rotation controller
* curl -k -v -XGET  -H "Accept: application/
json;as=Table;v=v1;g=meta.k8s.io,application/
json;as=Table;v=v1beta1;g=meta.k8s.io,application/json" -H
"User-Agent: kubectl/v1.19.0 (darwin/amd64) kubernetes/
e199641" 'https://127.0.0.1:55000/api/v1/namespaces/default/
pods?limit=500'
```

```
* GET https://127.0.0.1:55000/api/v1/namespaces/default/
pods?limit=500 200 OK in 19 milliseconds
* Response Headers:
    Cache-Control: no-cache, private
    Content-Type: application/json
...
```

As expected, it is a GET command to /api/v1/namespaces/default/
pods address for listing the pods in the default namespace. As you can
realize, the endpoints are structured with two main parts: API versions and
groups.

API Versioning

There are three levels of API versions in Kubernetes with the following
characteristics:

- **Stable**: Stable versions have the name vX where X is an
  integer such as v1. As expected, stable API endpoints
  provide well-established features that will live in the
  subsequent releases of Kubernetes.

- **Beta**: Beta API versions have a name containing beta such
  as v1beta1. The features and resources are well tested and
  enabled by default. However, the support for these APIs
  could be obsolete in the upcoming releases. Therefore, you
  should use beta APIs with great care in production.

- **Alpha**: Alpha API versions have a name containing
  alpha, such as v1alpha1. Alpha features are new and
  may contain bugs. More importantly, Kubernetes may
  drop the support or alter the API without considering
  backward compatibility. Therefore, you should only use
  alpha APIs for testing and not in production.

API Groups

API groups break the monolith structure of an API server and make enabling or disabling the groups individually. In Kubernetes, there are several API groups with two naming convention:

- The legacy core group has apiVersion: v1 and is located at /api/v1 with its historical reasons.

- All other groups are named with apiVersion: $GROUP_NAME/$VERSION and located at /apis/$GROUP_NAME/$VERSION. For instance, deployment objects are constructed as follows with the apiVersion of apps/v1.

Listing 4-3. Example deployment

```
apiVersion: apps/v1
kind: Deployment
metadata:
  name: nginx
spec:
  replicas: 5
  selector:
    matchLabels:
      app: nginx
  template:
    metadata:
      labels:
        app: nginx
    spec:
      containers:
      - name: nginx
        image: nginx:1.14
```

API endpoint for the deployment is `/apis/apps/v1/`
`↪namespaces/$NAMESPACE/deployments`, including the group name and
version.

Extending the Kubernetes API focuses on two parts: adding new
endpoints and adding custom implementation logic for the resources
located at endpoints. Now, let's continue with the two extension points of
the Kubernetes API.

Extension Points in Kubernetes API

Kubernetes API is a resource-oriented API, and the extension is possible by
creating custom resources. Custom resources can dynamically be added
or removed while the cluster is up and running. When a custom resource
is enabled, it has similar capabilities to a native resource such as pods.
Kubernetes provides two ways of adding custom resources.

CustomResourceDefinitions

`CustomResourceDefinition` (CRD) is a native Kubernetes API resource to
define custom resources. In a CRD, you represent a new custom resource
with its name, group, version, and schema. Kubernetes API server creates a
REST endpoint for your custom resource and handles API operations such
as create, read, update, and delete. The custom resource instances are
stored in `etcd` like all other Kubernetes resources.

API Server Aggregation

Each resource in Kubernetes has a REST endpoint to handle CRUD
operations. `APIService` is a native Kubernetes resource to register custom
resources with the group, version, and a back-end endpoint. You can claim
a URL path such as `/apis/k8s-extend.io/v1` and make `kube-apiserver`
delegate requests to your custom backend.

The main difference between the two methods is that CRDs extend the Kubernetes API by adding new resources inside the Kubernetes API. On the other hand, server aggregation creates new resources handled by an external server. The two approaches can be illustrated as follows in Figure 4-2.

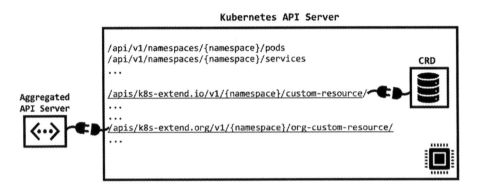

Figure 4-2. *Kubernetes API Extensions*

Custom resources with CRDs are structured data stored in Kubernetes API. However, their power comes from the *custom controllers*. Controllers act on the state of custom resources and take actions such as creation, deletion, or update. Custom resources with controllers are also mentioned as *operator pattern* first defined by CoreOs in 2016. You can create custom controllers to implement business logic based on the state stored in custom resources. Both custom controllers and aggregated servers need to communicate with the Kubernetes API server. Therefore, you need to develop applications in accordance with Kubernetes REST API. Luckily, you do not need to implement every resource and request from scratch as client libraries are available.

Kubernetes Client Libraries

Kubernetes client libraries implement native resources with requests and responses. In addition, they handle everyday tasks such as authentication, the discovery of credentials, and kubeconfig reading. There are officially supported client libraries for Go, Python, Java, Dotnet, JavaScript, and Haskell. In addition, there are many community-maintained client libraries with different coverage of native resources and focus areas.

Kubernetes maintains the list of client libraries in the official documentation; however, it is suggested to use Go or Python since they have the most active community. In addition, Kubernetes and its ecosystem are developed on Go language; thus, the Go client library is an indisputable winner. In the following exercise, you will connect to a Kubernetes cluster using the Go client library, namely, `client-go`.

EXERCISE: KUBERNETES GO CLIENT IN ACTION

In this exercise, you will create a custom watcher for secrets using `client-go`. We will start by creating a dependency file and source code. Then, we will build the binary with the help of cross-platform options in Go. Finally, you will run the custom watcher and see it in action.

Note   In order to continue this exercise, you need a running Kubernetes cluster and a `kubeconfig` to access. A local cluster created by `minikube` is sufficient for executing the steps.

---

1. Create a dependency file `go.mod` with the following content:

```
module secret-watcher
go 1.14
require (
      k8s.io/apimachinery v0.19.0
      k8s.io/client-go v0.19.0
)
```

go.mod file consists of the requirements for our application. The first one is apimachinery, and it is the library that provides resource definitions. The second is the client-go library, which includes authentication, utilities, and client commands.

2. Create a file secret_watcher.go with the following content:

```
package main

import (
  "context"
  "flag"
  "fmt"
  "path/filepath"
  "time"

  metav1 "k8s.io/apimachinery/pkg/apis/meta/v1"
  "k8s.io/client-go/kubernetes"
  "k8s.io/client-go/tools/clientcmd"
  "k8s.io/client-go/util/homedir"

  _ "k8s.io/client-go/plugin/pkg/client/auth"
)

func main() {
  // kubeconfig flag
  var kubeconfig *string
  if home := homedir.HomeDir(); home != "" {
    kubeconfig = flag.String("kubeconfig", filepath.
    Join(home, ".kube", "config"), "(optional) path to
    the kubeconfig file")
  } else {
    kubeconfig = flag.String("kubeconfig", "", "path to
    the kubeconfig file")
  }
  flag.Parse()
```

```
// create config
config, err := clientcmd.BuildConfigFromFlags("",
*kubeconfig)
if err != nil {
  panic(err.Error())
}

// create client set
clientset, err := kubernetes.NewForConfig(config)
if err != nil {
  panic(err.Error())
}

// watch for secrets
for {
  secrets, err := clientset.CoreV1().Secrets("").
  List(context.TODO(), metav1.ListOptions{})
  if err != nil {
    panic(err.Error())
  }
  fmt.Printf("There are %d secrets in the cluster\n",
  len(secrets.Items))
  time.Sleep(10 * time.Second)
}
}
```

It is the main file which we will build and run to communicate with the cluster. The function starts parsing the kubeconfig flag if the default directory is not used. Then it reads the kubeconfig using the client-go library. Following that, a clientset is created which consists of clients for native resources. In the end, all secrets are listed and the count is printed in an infinite loop.

3. Start a Go build environment in Docker with the following
    command:

    ```
    $ docker run -v "$(pwd)":/go/src/secret-watcher -it
    onuryilmaz/multi-platform-go-build:1.14-buster bash
    root@e45653990bb6:/go#
    ```

    The command will mount the current working directory and
    start an interactive bash inside the container.

4. Run the following command to build the binary:

    ```
    $ cd src/secret-watcher/
    $ export GOOS=darwin # for MacOS. Set to linux or windows
    based on your local operating system
    $ go build -v
    go: downloading k8s.io/apimachinery v0.19.0
    go: downloading k8s.io/client-go v0.19.0
    go: downloading github.com/google/gofuzz v1.1.0
    go: downloading gopkg.in/inf.v0 v0.9.1
    ...
    k8s.io/client-go/kubernetes/typed/storage/v1alpha1
    k8s.io/client-go/kubernetes/typed/storage/v1
    k8s.io/client-go/kubernetes/typed/storage/v1beta1
    k8s.io/client-go/kubernetes
    secret-watcher
    ```

    The output lists retrieving all the dependencies and, in the
    end, building the binary. Exit from the container to the local
    workstation with the exit command.

5. Run the secret-watcher binary, setting kubeconfig flag or
    leaving as empty to use the default location:

    ```
    ./secret-watcher
    There are 37 secrets in the cluster
    ```

```
There are 37 secrets in the cluster
There are 37 secrets in the cluster
...
```

The `secret-watcher` application lists all the secrets in the cluster in an infinite loop, as shown in the output. The successful run of the binary shows that we can create a custom Go application using the `client-go` library. In addition, it communicates with the cluster, which shows that cluster configuration, requests, and responses are working flawlessly.

In the following section, we will extend the Kubernetes API with custom resources and controllers. We will learn the basics of operator patterns and then create custom resources to expand the Kubernetes API. We will then understand the controller concept and make Kubernetes work for our custom resources and business logic.

Custom Resource Definitions and Controllers

`CustomResourceDefinition` (CRD) is the straightforward way of creating custom resources in Kubernetes API. With the new resources, Kubernetes API is extended to handle the REST operations and storage in `etcd`. It means that you can create, read, update, or delete the custom resources, and most importantly, you can create automation on them. Therefore, *the idea is to create custom resources for the business requirements not implemented in vanilla Kubernetes*. Let's assume you want to install a clustered and managed database on Kubernetes. You will deploy secrets, volumes, configurations, statefulsets, and many more Kubernetes resources. In addition, you want to run some business logic such as database initialization, migration, or upgrade for your database. Custom resources and the controllers are the design pattern to follow for managing such applications in a Kubernetes-native way. Let's start by creating some CRDs to define custom resources.

CRDs are similar to any other Kubernetes resources; they are declarative definitions for the desired state. In this case, the desired state is a new custom resource with a group name, version, scope, schema, and name. An example CRD for TimeseriesDB resources can be constructed as follows.

Listing 4-4. TimeseriesDB CRD

```
apiVersion: apiextensions.k8s.io/v1
kind: CustomResourceDefinition
metadata:
  name: timeseriesdbs.extend-k8s.io
spec:
  group: extend-k8s.io
  versions:
    - name: v1
      served: true
      storage: true
      schema:
        openAPIV3Schema:
          type: object
          properties:
            spec:
              type: object
              properties:
                dbType:
                  type: string
                replicas:
                  type: integer
```

```
        status:
          type: object
          properties:
            stage:
              type: string
            message:
              type: string
scope: Namespaced
names:
  plural: timeseriesdbs
  singular: timeseriesdb
  kind: TimeseriesDB
  shortNames:
  - tsdb
```

In the spec of a CRD, there are four blocks:

- group: Multiple custom resources can be grouped into a single Kubernetes API group. The field represents the name of the API group.

- versions: In Kubernetes, resources are versioned with changing schemas. In the CRD, the supported versions with their schema are provided.

- scope: Custom resource instances can be living in a Namespace or can be Cluster wide.

- names: Plural, singular, and kind fields are the names for the resource to use in REST endpoints, resource definition files, and kubectl commands.

Names of the CRD resources are defined in metadata.name, and it is in the pattern of <plural>.<group>. Also, Kubernetes stores structured data in custom resources with their custom fields. The fields' structure is specified in the schema field, and it is in the form of OpenAPI specification v3.0. Now, save the CRD in a file and deploy it to the cluster.

Listing 4-5. Deployment of CRD

```
$ kubectl apply -f tsdb-crd.yaml
customresourcedefinition.apiextensions.k8s.io/timeseriesdbs.
extend-k8s.io created
```

Now, you can see the `timeseriesdbs` is added to API resources in the cluster.

Listing 4-6. API resources listing

```
$ kubectl api-resources --output=name | grep timeseriesdbs
timeseriesdbs.extend-k8s.io
```

Besides, you can run `kubectl` commands and interact with the Kubernetes API for `TimeseriesDB` resources. Let's try it with some logging enabled.

Listing 4-7. `kubectl` custom resource listing

```
$ kubectl get timeseriesdb -v=6 | grep extend-k8s
Config loaded from file:  ...
Starting client certificate rotation controller
GET https://127.0.0.1:55000/api?timeout=32s 200 OK in 18
milliseconds
GET https://127.0.0.1:55000/apis?timeout=32s 200 OK in 6
milliseconds
GET https://127.0.0.1:55000/apis/extend-k8s.io/v1?timeout=32s
200 OK in 11 milliseconds
GET https://127.0.0.1:55000/apis/autoscaling/v1?timeout=32s 200
OK in 10 milliseconds
...
```

```
GET https://127.0.0.1:55000/apis/storage.k8s.io/
v1beta1?timeout=32s 200 OK in 20 milliseconds
GET https://127.0.0.1:55000/apis/extend-k8s.io/v1/namespaces/
default/timeseriesdbs?limit=500 200 OK in 4 milliseconds
No resources found in default namespace.
```

Note   If you do not see API retrieval logs, it is due to the fact that kubectl caches them. You can clear the cache directory located at $HOME/.kube/cache and rerun the command.

In the logs, kubectl first connects to api and apis endpoints to discover the available API groups and versions. The API discovery results are locally cached so that in the second run, kubectl will directly call /apis/extend-k8s.io/v1/namespaces/default/timeseriesdbs.

Kubernetes API is extended with the creation of CRD; thus, both the API server and client tools are ready to work with new resources. As expected, there are no resources for TimeseriesDB. Now, let's continue with creating the custom resources in the cluster.

TimeseriesDB or any custom resource you will create is not different than native Kubernetes resources such as pods or secrets. For the timeseriesdbs.extend-k8s.io CRD and the v1 schema, you can create the following resource.

Listing 4-8. TimeseriesDB example

```
apiVersion: extend-k8s.io/v1
kind: TimeseriesDB
metadata:
  name: example-tsdb
spec:
  dbType: InfluxDB
  replicas: 4
```

```
status:
  stage: Created
  message: New TimeseriesDB
```

example-tsdb is a definition for creating an *InfluxDB* database
with four replicas. The status fields explain the current situation of the
resource. Now, let's match the CRD and example resource fields visually in
Figure 4-3.

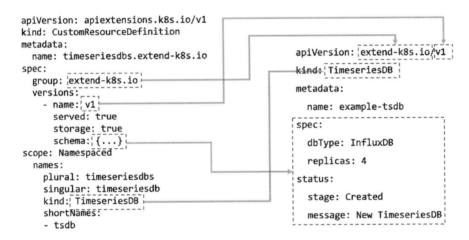

Figure 4-3. *CRD and custom resource*

You can deploy the resource to cluster with the following command.

Listing 4-9. Custom resource deployment

```
$ kubectl apply -f example-tsdb.yaml
timeseriesdb.extend-k8s.io/example-tsdb created
```

You can also use the shortNames defined in the CRD for accessing the
resources.

Listing 4-10. Custom resource listing

```
$ kubectl get tsdb
NAME            AGE
example-tsdb    1m
```

Now, we have a custom resource to manage our time-series databases. The critical question is, now, who will create and manage the four instances of *InfluxDB* into our cluster. Similarly, who will upgrade the database when a new version is released? In other words, there needs to be an *operator* to create, update, delete, and manage the applications.

Operator Pattern in Kubernetes

Kubernetes API stores and serves custom resources. On the other hand, operators are the software extensions to create and manage applications defined in the custom resources. The motivation behind *software operators* is to replace the knowledge and experience of *human operators*. In the traditional approach, the operations team *knows* how to deploy and manage the applications. They watch for specific metrics or dashboards to track the status of the overall system and take actions if necessary. In the cloud-native world, you are expected to use automation to take care of such operations.

Operators are the pattern to implement human knowledge and tasks into code. The pattern is well integrated into Kubernetes since it follows the controller extension pattern that is prevailing in Kubernetes. There are four main levels for an operator to manage production-ready cloud-native applications:

- **Installation**: Automated installation of the application with the desired state defined in the custom resource.

- **Upgrade**: Automated and user-triggered upgrade of the application with minimum user interaction.

117

- **Lifecycle Management**: Initialization, backup, and failure recovery for the applications with decision rules and automation.

- **Monitoring and Scalability**: Monitor and analyze the metrics and alerts for the application. Take automated actions for scaling, scheduling, and rebalancing when necessary.

Operators are deployed to clusters with the CustomResourceDefinition and the associated controllers. Controllers run inside Kubernetes as containerized applications, most commonly as a deployment. The operator application interacts with the Kubernetes API; therefore, it is suggested to use a programming language that can act as a Kubernetes client. Open source and community-maintained operators are shared in OperatorHub, and it has 175 operators available to use. If you plan to deploy a popular database to Kubernetes such as etcd, MongoDB, PostgreSQL, or CockroachDB, you should check the operators in OperatorHub. Using a ready-made operator with community support helps you save time and money; therefore, it is valuable.

If you want to develop your own operator, there are two essential tools to consider:

- **Operator SDK:** It is a part of the Operator Framework to create Kubernetes-native applications in an effective and automated approach. The SDK provides tooling to build, test, package, and deploy operators to the cluster. It is possible to develop in Go, Ansible, or Helm charts in Operator SDK.

- **kubebuilder:** It is a framework for building Kubernetes APIs using CRDs. It focuses on velocity and reduced complexity to create and deploy extensions to Kubernetes API. The tool generates clients, interfaces, and webhooks for custom resources in Go. It also generates the resources necessary to deploy operators to the cluster. Next, we will focus on the kubebuilder framework owing to its two essential features: vicinity to Kubernetes community and enhanced developer experience.

kubebuilder Framework

kubebuilder is a framework to initialize, generate, and deploy Kubernetes-native API extension code to clusters. The framework is *batteries included* so that the created projects have the testing environment, deployment files, and container specifications. This section will step by step generate a project for TimeseriesDB custom resource using the framework and see it in action.

Note   The rest of the section is to get your hands dirty with the following prerequisites: Go version v1.14+, Docker version 17.03+, access to a fresh Kubernetes cluster, and kubectl and kustomize.

Let's start by installing the kubebuilder binary to the local workstation.

Listing 4-11. kubebuilder installation

```
$ export os=$(go env GOOS)
$ export arch=$(go env GOARCH)

$ curl -L https://go.kubebuilder.io/dl/2.3.1/${os}/${arch} |
tar -xz -C /tmp/

$ sudo mv /tmp/kubebuilder_2.3.1_${os}_${arch} /usr/local/
kubebuilder

$export PATH=$PATH:/usr/local/kubebuilder/bin
```

The commands download the binary for your operating system and install it to your PATH environment variable. Next, it is time to create a new Go project.

Listing 4-12. Initializing a project

```
$ mkdir -p $GOPATH/src/extend-k8s.io/timeseries-operator
$ cd $GOPATH/src/extend-k8s.io/timeseries-operator
$ kubebuilder init --domain extend-k8s.io

Writing scaffold for you to edit...
Get controller runtime:
  go get sigs.k8s.io/controller-runtime@v0.5.0
go: downloading sigs.k8s.io/controller-runtime v0.5.0
go: downloading k8s.io/apimachinery v0.17.2
...
go fmt ./...
go vet ./...
go build -o bin/manager main.go
Next: define a resource with:
  kubebuilder create api
```

The commands create a folder in GOPATH, and then kubebuilder initializes by creating a scaffold project. Check the contents of the folder with the following command.

Listing 4-13. Project structure

```
$ tree -a
.
├── .gitignore
├── Dockerfile
├── Makefile
├── PROJECT
```

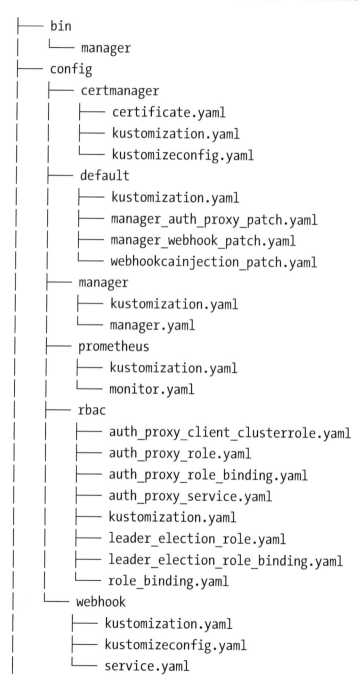

```
├── bin
│   └── manager
├── config
│   ├── certmanager
│   │   ├── certificate.yaml
│   │   ├── kustomization.yaml
│   │   └── kustomizeconfig.yaml
│   ├── default
│   │   ├── kustomization.yaml
│   │   ├── manager_auth_proxy_patch.yaml
│   │   ├── manager_webhook_patch.yaml
│   │   └── webhookcainjection_patch.yaml
│   ├── manager
│   │   ├── kustomization.yaml
│   │   └── manager.yaml
│   ├── prometheus
│   │   ├── kustomization.yaml
│   │   └── monitor.yaml
│   ├── rbac
│   │   ├── auth_proxy_client_clusterrole.yaml
│   │   ├── auth_proxy_role.yaml
│   │   ├── auth_proxy_role_binding.yaml
│   │   ├── auth_proxy_service.yaml
│   │   ├── kustomization.yaml
│   │   ├── leader_election_role.yaml
│   │   ├── leader_election_role_binding.yaml
│   │   └── role_binding.yaml
│   └── webhook
│       ├── kustomization.yaml
│       ├── kustomizeconfig.yaml
│       └── service.yaml
```

```
├──── go.mod
├──── go.sum
├──── hack
│       └──── boilerplate.go.txt
└──── main.go
```

```
9 directories, 31 files
```

kubebuilder initializes the project with minimal resources to build and run an operator. Most of the files are in the config folder with the format of kustomize, a template-free way of customization integrated into kubectl.

Add the TimeseriesDB API to the project by creating the resource and controller.

Listing 4-14. Adding new API

```
$ kubebuilder create api --group operator --version v1 --kind
TimeseriesDB
Create Resource [y/n]
y
Create Controller [y/n]
y
Writing scaffold for you to edit...
api/v1/timeseriesdb_types.go
controllers/timeseriesdb_controller.go
Running make:
make
...bin/controller-gen object:headerFile="hack/boilerplate.
go.txt" paths="./..."
go fmt ./...
go vet ./...
go build -o bin/manager main.go
```

A boilerplate resource and controller are added to the project. Let's first check the resource definition located at /api/v1/timeseriesdb_ types.go.

Listing 4-15. Boilerplate TimeseriesDB resource

```
type TimeseriesDBSpec struct {
    ...
    Foo string `json:"foo,omitempty"`
}

type TimeseriesDBStatus struct {
    ...
}

// +kubebuilder:object:root=true

// TimeseriesDB is the Schema for the timeseriesdbs API
type TimeseriesDB struct {
    metav1.TypeMeta   `json:",inline"`
    metav1.ObjectMeta `json:"metadata,omitempty"`

    Spec   TimeseriesDBSpec   `json:"spec,omitempty"`
    Status TimeseriesDBStatus `json:"status,omitempty"`
}
```

Update the TimeseriesDBSpec and TimeseriesDBStatus with the following Go structs to remove example fields and store actual data.

Listing 4-16. TimeseriesDBSpec with actual fields

```
// TimeseriesDBSpec defines the desired state of TimeseriesDB
type TimeseriesDBSpec struct {
    DBType   string `json:"dbType,omitempty"`
    Replicas int    `json:"replicas,omitempty"`
}
```

Listing 4-17. TimeseriesDBStatus with actual fields

```
// TimeseriesDBStatus defines the observed state of
TimeseriesDB
type TimeseriesDBStatus struct {
    Status  string `json:"status,omitempty"`
    Message string `json:"message,omitempty"`
}
```

In addition, change the kubebuilder flags to set status as a subresource just before the TimeseriesDB definition.

Listing 4-18. Status subresource flag

```
// +kubebuilder:object:root=true
// +kubebuilder:subresource:status
```

Check Reconcile method of controller code located at /controllers/timeseriesdb_controller.go.

Listing 4-19. Boilerplate TimeseriesDB controller

```
func (r *TimeseriesDBReconciler) Reconcile(req ctrl.Request)
(ctrl.Result, error) {
    _ = context.Background()
    _ = r.Log.WithValues("timeseriesdb", req.NamespacedName)

    // your logic here

    return ctrl.Result{}, nil
}
```

The Reconcile method of the controller will be called for every transaction of TimeseriesDB instances in Kubernetes API. Update the function with the following content.

Listing 4-20. Updated controller

```
func (r *TimeseriesDBReconciler) Reconcile(req ctrl.Request)
(ctrl.Result, error) {
    ctx := context.Background()
    log := r.Log.WithValues("timeseriesdb", req.
    NamespacedName)

    timeseriesdb := new(operatorv1.TimeseriesDB)

    if err := r.Client.Get(ctx, req.NamespacedName,
    timeseriesdb); err != nil {
        return ctrl.Result{}, client.IgnoreNotFound(err)
    }

    log = log.WithValues("dbType", timeseriesdb.Spec.DBType,
    "replicas", timeseriesdb.Spec.Replicas)

    if timeseriesdb.Status.Status == "" || timeseriesdb.
    Status.Message == "" {
        timeseriesdb.Status = operatorv1.
        TimeseriesDBStatus{Status: "Initialized", Message:
        "Database creation is in progress"}
        err := r.Status().Update(ctx, timeseriesdb)
        if err != nil {
            log.Error(err, "status update failed")
            return ctrl.Result{}, err
        }
        log.Info("status updated")
    }

    return ctrl.Result{}, nil
}
```

The updated reconciler method shows how to retrieve `TimeseriesDB` instances using clients generated by `kubebuilder`. The fields of the retrieved objects are printed to the output. In addition, the status part is filled if empty, and the resource is updated in the cluster.

Run `make` command to generate clients and sample files with the updated `TimeseriesDB` resource.

Listing 4-21. Code generation after resource update

```
$ make
.../controller-gen object:headerFile="hack/boilerplate.go.txt"
paths="./..."
go fmt ./...
go vet ./...
go build -o bin/manager main.go
```

`kubebuilder` platform uses the `controller-gen` tool for generating utility code and Kubernetes resource files in YAML format.

Install the CRD to the cluster and run the controller locally.

Listing 4-22. Running the controller locally

```
$ make install run

.../controller-gen "crd:trivialVersions=true"
rbac:roleName=manager-role webhook paths="./..." output:crd:art
ifacts:config=config/crd/bases
...
kustomize build config/crd | kubectl apply -f -
customresourcedefinition.apiextensions.k8s.io/timeseriesdbs.
operator.extend-k8s.io created
...
.../controller-gen object:headerFile="hack/boilerplate.go.txt"
paths="./..."
```

```
go fmt ./...
go vet ./...
go run ./main.go
...
INFO    controller-runtime.metrics      metrics server is
starting to listen    {"addr": ":8080"}
INFO    setup   starting manager
INFO    controller-runtime.manager      starting metrics server
{"path": "/metrics"}
INFO    controller-runtime.controller   Starting
EventSource   {"controller": "timeseriesdb", "source": "kind
source: /, Kind="}
INFO    controller-runtime.controller   Starting Controller
{"controller": "timeseriesdb"}
INFO    controller-runtime.controller   Starting workers
{"controller": "timeseriesdb", "worker count": 1}
```

In the logs, the CRD is installed, and then the controller code started using Go commands. Metrics server, events source, controllers, and workers began in the listed order, and our controller is now ready, waiting for the resource changes.

Update the sample TimeseriesDB instances located at /config/sample/operator_v1_timeseriesdb.yaml with the following content.

Listing 4-23. Example TimeseriesDB instance

```
apiVersion: operator.extend-k8s.io/v1
kind: TimeseriesDB
metadata:
  name: timeseriesdb-sample
spec:
  dbType: Prometheus
  replicas: 5
```

In another terminal, deploy the sample custom resource to the cluster.

Listing 4-24. Deploying example `TimeseriesDB` instance

```
$ kubectl apply -f config/samples/
timeseriesdb.operator.extend-k8s.io/timeseriesdb-sample created
```

In the terminal where the controller is running, you should see the following two lines now.

Listing 4-25. Controller logs after custom resource creation

```
INFO    controllers.TimeseriesDB        status
updated  {"timeseriesdb": "default/timeseriesdb-sample",
"dbType": "Prometheus", "replicas": 5}
DEBUG   controller-runtime.controller    Successfully
Reconciled {"controller": "timeseriesdb", "request":
"default/timeseriesdb-sample"}
```

It shows that the `Reconcile` method of the controller is called with the creation of the resource. Let's check if the status is updated correctly.

Listing 4-26. Custom resource status

```
$ kubectl describe timeseriesdb timeseriesdb-sample
Name:         timeseriesdb-sample
Namespace:    default
...
Spec:
  Db Type:    Prometheus
  Replicas:   5
Status:
  Message:  Database creation is in progress
  Status:    Initialized
Events:       <none>
```

The controller updates the status fields, and it shows that the controller is not in a read-only mode and it can make changes to the resources.

After creating an operator from scratch using the `kubebuilder` framework, you have an impression of how to extend Kubernetes API with custom resources and controllers. It is worth mentioning that while developing operators, there are three essential points to be considered:

- **Declarative**: Kubernetes has a declarative API, and its resources should be the same. Your custom resources and controllers around them should be reading the `spec` and updating the `status` fields only. If you find yourself changing the `spec` in a controller, you need to revise your custom resources and controller logic.

- **Idempotent**: The changes done by the controller should be idempotent and atomic. It protects you from creating a complete database from scratch when the operator pod is restarted in the middle of a reconciliation.

- **Resistant to Errors**: Controllers create resources inside or outside the cluster, and thus, it is open to having errors, timeouts, or cancellations. You need to consider each action of the controller and its potential failure. The Kubernetes-native approach is to retry with a backoff policy, update the resource's status, and publish events if necessary.

Next, we will continue with the second extension point in Kubernetes API to create new resources handled by an external server.

Aggregated API and Extension Servers

The aggregation layer extends Kubernetes with additional APIs to provide beyond what the Kubernetes API server offers. The main difference between CRD and operator pattern is that *new resources are not stored in Kubernetes API*. The requests of the resources are directed to an external server, and responses are collected. While the approach increases flexibility, it also increases operational complexity. There are three essential elements of extending the Kubernetes API by aggregation:

- **Aggregation Layer**: The layer runs inside kube-apiserver and proxies the requests for the new API types.

- **APIService Resources**: New API types are registered by APIService resources dynamically.

- **Extension API Servers**: Extension API servers respond to the requests proxied over the aggregation layer.

We can illustrate a request's flow starting in the Kubernetes API and ending in the extension API server in Figure 4-4. The journey of incoming requests begins with the authentication and authorization of the user. Then, the aggregation layer directs the request to the extension API server. In the extension server, the incoming request is authenticated against the API server. In other words, the extension API server checks whether the requests are coming from the Kubernetes API server. Then, the extension server validates the authorization of the request with the original user. Finally, if the request passes all stages, then it is executed and stored in the extension server. The request flow shows that extending the Kubernetes API server with an extension server follows the webhook design pattern.

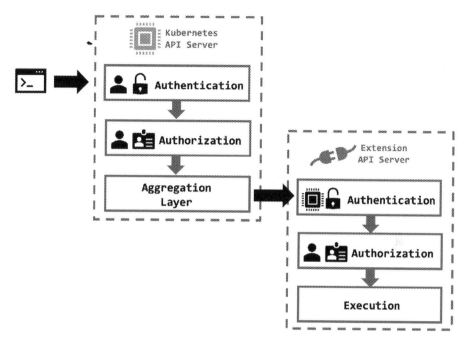

Figure 4-4. *Aggregated API request flow*

Dynamic configuration of extension servers and new resources are controlled by APIService resources. APIService resources consist of an API group, version, and an endpoint for the extension server. An example APIService resource to extend Kubernetes API for backup.extend-k8s.io group and v1 version can be constructed as follows.

Listing 4-27. Example APIService resource

```
apiVersion: apiregistration.k8s.io/v1
kind: APIService
metadata:
  name: v1.backup.extend-k8s.io
spec:
  version: v1
  group: backup.extend-k8s.io
```

```
groupPriorityMinimum: 2000
service:
  name: extension-server
  namespace: kube-extensions
versionPriority: 10
caBundle: "LSOtL...LSOK"
```

The definition does not specify the actual names of custom resources. Instead, the aggregation layer redirects all requests coming to /apis/ backup.extend-k8s.io/v1/ endpoint. The extension server manages all the custom resources in the API groups. The extension server is specified as a Kubernetes service with its name and namespace. By default, the HTTPS port of the service is used, and communication is handled over TLS. The extension server is required to run with a cert signed by the CA certificate specified in caBundle.

An extension API server's development is almost as complicated as developing a Kubernetes API server, namely, kube-apiserver. For a concrete example of a full-fetch, reference implementation, you can check sample-apiserver repository of Kubernetes. The recommended way of using sample-apiserver is to fork the repository, modify the API types, and frequently rebase to follow the improvements and bug fixes.

In this section, we will generate and deploy an extension API server from scratch using apiserver-builder. It is a complete framework for developing an API server, client libraries, and installation resources. We will use the tool to initialize a project, adding custom resource groups and versions, code generation, and deployment to the cluster.

Note   The steps in this section require the following to be installed in addition to a running Kubernetes cluster: Go v1.14+, Docker version 17.03+, and OpenSSL 1.1.1g+.

First, let's install the apiserver-boot tool with its latest available release.

Listing 4-28. apiserver-boot installation

```
$ export os=$(go env GOOS)
$ mkdir -p /tmp/apiserver
$ cd /tmp/apiserver
$ curl  --output /tmp/apiserver/apiserver-builder-alpha.tar.
gz -L https://github.com/kubernetes-sigs/apiserver-builder-
alpha/releases/download/v2.0.0-alpha.0/apiserver-builder-alpha-
v2.0.0-alpha.0-${os}-amd64.tar.gz

$ tar -xf /tmp/apiserver/      apiserver-builder-alpha.tar.gz
$ chmod +x /tmp/apiserver/bin/apiserver-boot

$ mkdir -p /usr/local/apiserver-builder/bin
$ mv /tmp/apiserver/bin/apiserver-boot /usr/local/apiserver-
builder/bin/apiserver-boot
$ export PATH=$PATH:/usr/local/apiserver-builder/bin
```

You can verify the installation by running the following command.

Listing 4-29. apiserver-boot version check

```
$ apiserver-boot version
Version: version.Version{ApiserverBuilderVersion:"8f12f3e43",
KubernetesVendor:"kubernetes-1.19.2", GitCommit:"8f12f3e43cb0a
75c82e8a6b316772a230f5fd471", BuildDate:"2020-11-04-20:35:32",
GoOs:"darwin", GoArch:"amd64"}
```

Let's start with creating a folder in GOPATH.

Listing 4-30. Go project initialization

```
$ mkdir -p $GOPATH/src/extend-k8s.io/timeseries-apiserver
$ cd $GOPATH/src/extend-k8s.io/timeseries-apiserver
```

Create a scaffold API server using `apiserver-boot`.

Listing 4-31. API server initialization

```
$ apiserver-boot init repo --domain extend-k8s.io
Writing scaffold for you to edit...
```

Now, check the generated files with the following command.

Listing 4-32. Folder structure

```
$ tree -a
.
├── .gitignore
├── BUILD.bazel
├── Dockerfile
├── Makefile
├── PROJECT
├── WORKSPACE
├── bin
├── cmd
│   ├── apiserver
│   │   └── main.go
│   └── manager
│       └── main.go -> ../../main.go
├── go.mod
├── hack
│   └── boilerplate.go.txt
```

```
├── main.go
└── pkg
    └── apis
        └── doc.go
```

```
7 directories, 12 files
```

The generated code is a basic API server with tooling such as Makefile and bazel files.

Add a custom resource and controller to the extension server with the following command.

Listing 4-33. Adding custom resource

```
$ apiserver-boot create group version resource --group backup
--version v1 --kind TimeseriesDBBackup
Create Resource [y/n]
y
Create Controller [y/n]
y
Writing scaffold for you to edit...
controllers/backup/timeseriesdbbackup_controller.go
```

Run code generation tool to ensure that new resources and controllers work as expected.

Listing 4-34. Code generation for new resource and controller

```
$  make generate
...controller-gen object:headerFile="hack/boilerplate.go.txt"
paths="./..."
```

First, export $REPOSITORY environment variable as your Docker repository and then build the container image for the extension server.

Listing 4-35. Container build

```
$ apiserver-boot build container --image $REPOSITORY/
timeseries-apiserver:v1

Will build docker Image from directory /var/folders/nn/.../T/
apiserver-boot-build-container656172154
Writing the Dockerfile.
Building binaries for Linux amd64.
CGO_ENABLED=0
GOOS=linux
GOARCH=amd64
go build -o /var/folders/nn/.../T/apiserver-boot-build-
container656172154/apiserver cmd/apiserver/main.go
go build -o /var/folders/nn/.../T/apiserver-boot-build-
container656172154/controller-manager cmd/manager/main.go

Building the docker Image using /var/folders/nn/.../T/
apiserver-boot-build-container656172154/Dockerfile.

docker build -t $REPOSITORY     /timeseries-apiserver:v1 /var/
folders/nn/../T/apiserver-boot-build-container656172154
Sending build context to Docker daemon   102.2MB
Step 1/5 : FROM ubuntu:14.04
 ---> df043b4f0cf1
Step 2/5 : RUN apt-get update
 ---> Using cache
 ---> 60dfe53c07c6
Step 3/5 : RUN apt-get install -y ca-certificates
 ---> Using cache
 ---> ff5f3be9ac8d
Step 4/5 : ADD apiserver .
 ---> 3778467102f7
```

```
Step 5/5 : ADD controller-manager .
 ---> 32672f63fd9b
Successfully built 32672f63fd9b
Successfully tagged $REPOSITORY/timeseries-apiserver:v1
```

Push the Docker container to the registry to use inside Kubernetes clusters.

Listing 4-36. Container push

```
$ docker push $REPOSITORY/timeseries-apiserver:v1
```

Deploy the extension API server with the following command.

Listing 4-37. Deployment of extension server

```
$ apiserver-boot run in-cluster --name timeseriesdb-api
--namespace default --image $REPOSITORY/timeseries-apiserver:
v1 --build-image=false

openssl req -x509 -newkey rsa:2048 -addext basicConstraints=
critical,CA:TRUE,pathlen:1 -keyout config/certificates/
apiserver_ca.key -out config/certificates/apiserver_ca.crt
-days 365 -nodes -subj /C=un/ST=st/L=l/O=o/OU=ou/
CN=timeseriesdb-api-certificate-authority
Generating a RSA private key
.+++++
..............................+++++
writing new private key to 'config/certificates/apiserver_ca.key'
...

Adding APIs:
    backup.v1
...
```

```
kubectl apply -f config
deployment.apps/timeseriesdb-api-apiserver created
secret/timeseriesdb-api created
service/timeseriesdb-api created
apiservice.apiregistration.k8s.io/v1.backup.extend-k8s.io
created
deployment.apps/timeseriesdb-api-controller created
statefulset.apps/etcd created
service/etcd-svc created
clusterrole.rbac.authorization.k8s.io/timeseriesdb-api-
apiserver-auth-reader created
clusterrolebinding.rbac.authorization.k8s.io/timeseriesdb-api-
apiserver-auth-reader created
clusterrolebinding.rbac.authorization.k8s.io/timeseriesdb-api-
apiserver-auth-delegator created
clusterrole.rbac.authorization.k8s.io/timeseriesdb-api-
controller created
clusterrolebinding.rbac.authorization.k8s.io/timeseriesdb-api-
controller created
```

The command handles a series of automation to create TLS certificates, adding the APIs, and deploying a long list of Kubernetes YAML files. Now, it is time to check whether the custom resource APIs are enabled and running as expected.

Let's start by describing the new APIService resource.

Listing 4-38. APIService status

```
$ kubectl describe apiservice v1.backup.extend-k8s.io
Name:         v1.backup.extend-k8s.io
Namespace:
...
Status:
```

```
Conditions:
    ...
    Message:              all checks passed
    Reason:               Passed
    Status:               True
    Type:                 Available
Events:                   <none>
```

Message field indicates that all checks passed, and also, the APIService is listed as Available. Create a sample TimeseriesDBBackup resource with the following content in example-tsdb-backup.yaml.

Listing 4-39. Example TimeseriesDBBackup

```
apiVersion: backup.extend-k8s.io/v1
kind: TimeseriesDBBackup
metadata:
  name: example-tsdb-backup
```

Deploy the example resource to the cluster and retrieve it back.

Listing 4-40. Create and read of the custom resource

```
$ kubectl apply -f example-tsdb-backup.yaml
timeseriesdbbackup.backup.extend-k8s.io/example-tsdb-backup
created

$ kubectl get TimeseriesDBBackups
NAME                    CREATED AT
example-tsdb-backup     2021-07-28T09:05:00Z
```

The outputs show that we can interact with the Kubernetes API for the custom resource extended by aggregated API.

The last step will be going one level more to check the extended resources' physical data in etcd. Kubernetes API server uses etcd as its database. Similarly, the extension API server interacts with its database to store the custom resources. etcd is deployed next to the extension API server, and it should have a pod running and accessible.

Listing 4-41. Access to etcd

```
$ kubectl exec -it etcd-0 -- sh
/ # ETCDCTL_API=3 etcdctl get --prefix /registry
/registry/sample-apiserver/backup.extend-k8s.io/
timeseriesdbbackups/example-tsdb-backup
{"kind":"TimeseriesDBBackup","apiVersion":"backup.extend-k8s.
io/v1","metadata":{"name":"example-tsdb-backup","uid":"...",
"creationTimestamp":"...","annotations":{"kubectl.kubernetes.
io/last-applied-configuration":"{\"apiVersion\":\"backup.
extend-k8s.io/v1\",\"kind\":\"TimeseriesDBBackup\",\"metadata\"
:{\"annotations\":{},\"name\":\"example-tsdb-backup\"}}\n"}},
"spec":{},"status":{}}
```

The data from etcd shows that the extension API server stores TimeseriesDBBackup instances. Also, using kubectl shows that Kubernetes API is extended with the aggregated API method.

Compared to using CRDs, creating and deploying a stand-alone server to handle API requests is not straightforward. However, extending the Kubernetes API with aggregated servers has the two following benefits over CRDs: more flexible validation checks over resources and protocol buffer support for clients. On the other hand, there are three essential points to consider while deploying an extension server:

- **New Points of Failure**: Aggregated API server runs on its own with the business logic and requirements. It should be designed well and operated with great care not to have a single point of failure in the cluster.

- **Storage**: Aggregated API servers can choose how to store the data. Initialization, backup, recovery, and storage capacity should be taken into consideration.

- **Security and Auditing**: Authentication, authorization, and auditing setup of the aggregated servers should align with the primary API server.

Key Takeaways

- Kubernetes API is the core fabric of the system, and all operations on the cluster are handled as requests to the API server.

- `CustomResourceDefinition` (CRD) is the straightforward way of adding new custom resources to Kubernetes API. It handles the REST operations and storage of the resources created by CRDs.

- When custom resources are combined with custom controllers, it is possible to implement human knowledge and tasks into code, namely, the operator pattern.

- The aggregation layer extends Kubernetes with additional APIs to provide beyond what the Kubernetes API server offers. Kubernetes API proxies the requests of the aggregated API resources.

In the following chapter, we will extend the Kubernetes scheduling with running multiple schedulers and developing custom ones.

CHAPTER 5

Scheduling Extensions

Action expresses priorities.

—Mahatma Gandhi
Indian lawyer, politician, social activist, and writer

The scheduler is a core part of Kubernetes to assign workload to the nodes in the cluster. The assignment action is based on priorities and rules set by cluster admins and operators. This chapter will focus on extending the Kubernetes scheduler by creating custom schedulers and developing extensions. At the end of this chapter, you will run multiple schedulers simultaneously in the cluster. In addition, you will intervene in the scheduling decisions by creating scheduler extenders.

Let's start with an overview of the Kubernetes scheduler and its extension points.

Kubernetes Scheduler Overview

Kubernetes scheduler runs in the control plane and assigns pods to the nodes. The default behavior is to balance resource utilization of nodes while applying the rules and priorities of resources in the cluster.

© Onur Yilmaz 2021
O. Yilmaz, *Extending Kubernetes*, https://doi.org/10.1007/978-1-4842-7095-0_5

The principle of scheduler follows the controller design pattern of Kubernetes. It watches for the newly created pods and finds the best node in the cluster.

Let's see the Kubernetes scheduler in action by creating a multi-node cluster from scratch and a pod.

Listing 5-1. Starting a multi-node local cluster

```
$ minikube start --nodes 5
```

The command will create a local cluster with five nodes which you can list with the following command.

Listing 5-2. Node listing

```
$ kubectl get nodes
NAME            STATUS   ROLES     AGE      VERSION
minikube        Ready    master    7m17s    v1.19.2
minikube-m02    Ready    <none>    5m43s    v1.19.2
minikube-m03    Ready    <none>    4m10s    v1.19.2
minikube-m04    Ready    <none>    2m22s    v1.19.2
minikube-m05    Ready    <none>    34s      v1.19.2
```

Now, let's create a pod and wait until it is running.

Listing 5-3. Pod creation

```
$ kubectl run nginx-1 --image=nginx
pod/nginx-1 created
$ kubectl get pods -w
NAME      READY   STATUS             RESTARTS   AGE
nginx-1   0/1     Pending            0          0s
nginx-1   0/1     Pending            0          0s
nginx-1   0/1     ContainerCreating  0          0s
nginx-1   1/1     Running            0          16s
```

You will see Pending, ContainerCreating, and Running stages in a couple of seconds. The vital step for scheduling is Pending. It indicates that Kubernetes API accepts the pod, but it is not yet scheduled to a cluster node. Let's check for the events to find any information related to scheduling.

Listing 5-4. Event listing

```
$ kubectl get events
...
2m54s        Normal    Scheduled                    pod/nginx-1
        Successfully assigned default/nginx-1 to minikube-m05
...
```

You will see that the kube-scheduler has selected the minikube-m05 node. Let's deep dive into the internals of kube-scheduler and learn more about how the decision is made.

Scheduling Framework

The scheduling framework is the architecture of Kubernetes scheduler. It is a pluggable framework where plugins implement the scheduling features. There are multiple steps in a sequential workflow in the framework, as illustrated in Figure 5-1. Workflow is mainly divided into two as *scheduling* and *binding*. Scheduling focuses on finding the best node, while binding handles Kubernetes API operations to finalize scheduling.

145

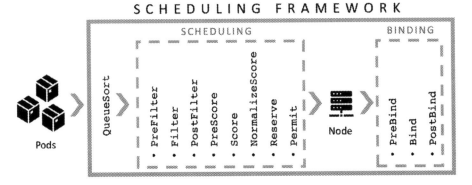

Figure 5-1. *Scheduling framework*

Each step has self-explanatory names, but there are some essential points to consider:

- QueueSort: Sort the pods to be scheduled in the waiting queue of the kube-scheduler.

- PreFilter: Check the conditions and the information of the pods related to the scheduling cycle.

- Filter: Filter the nodes to find a list of suitable nodes for the pod by using plugins and calling external scheduler extenders.

- PostFilter: It is an optional step to run if there are no feasible nodes. In a typical scenario, PostFilter will result in preemption of other pods to open up some space for scheduling.

- PreScore: Create a shareable state for scoring plugins.

- Score/Prioritize: Rank the filtered nodes by calling each scoring plugins and scheduler extenders.

- NormalizeScore: Combine the scores from multiple sources and compute a final ranking. The node with the highest weighted score will win the pod.

- `Reserve/Unreserve`: It is an optional step to inform plugins about a selected node.

- `Permit`: Approve, deny, or pause (with a timeout) the scheduling decision.

- `PreBind`: Perform any work required before the pod is bound to the node, such as provisioning a network volume and mounting it.

- `Bind`: The step is handled by only one plugin since it requires sending the decision to Kubernetes API.

- `PostBind`: It is an optional and informational step to inform the result of the binding cycle.

One plugin can register at multiple workflow points and perform scheduling subtasks. Although the framework and plugins create an open architecture, all plugins are compiled into the `kube-scheduler` binary. You can check the list of the available plugins from the reference documentation. It is the ultimate knowledge if you are looking to change the configuration of the `kube-scheduler` running in the control plane.

We have seen the scheduler in action and had a glimpse into its architecture. Now we will continue with defining the extension points and how to use them.

Extension Points

You can customize or extend the Kubernetes scheduler with four principal methods.

The first way is to clone and modify the upstream `kube-scheduler` code. Then you need to compile, containerize, and run instead of the `kube-scheduler` deployment in the control plane. However, it is not so straightforward and comes with a massive effort of lining up changes to upstream code in the next versions.

The second way is developing plugins for scheduling framework inside kube-scheduler. It is not *hacky* as the first approach, but again, it requires as much effort as the first one, because you need to update, compile, and maintain the changes of the upstream kube-scheduler repository.

The third approach is running a separate scheduler in the cluster along with the default one. There is a particular field in PodSpec to define the scheduler: schedulerName. If the field is empty, then it is set to the default-scheduler and handled by kube-scheduler. Thus, it is possible to run a second scheduler and specify it in the schedulerName field. Then, the custom scheduler will assign the pods to the nodes. This approach implements the controller Kubernetes design pattern. It will *watch* for the pods with the specific schedulerName and assign a node to them.

The fourth and the last way is developing and running scheduler extenders. Scheduler extenders are external servers, and Kubernetes scheduler calls them at specific steps of the scheduling framework. The approach is similar to the scheduling framework plugins, but the extenders are external services with HTTP endpoints. Thus, the extenders implement the webhook Kubernetes design pattern.

The first two extension methods are not actual extension points since they modify the vanilla Kubernetes components. Therefore, in this chapter, we will focus on the last two ways: multiple schedulers and scheduler extenders. We can illustrate the interaction of these two methods with the Kubernetes scheduler in Figure 5-2.

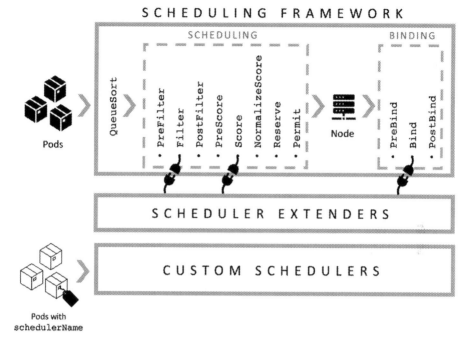

Figure 5-2. *Kubernetes scheduler extension points*

Three stages have interaction with scheduler extenders: Filter, Prioritize, and Bind. Therefore, it is beneficial to use extenders to operate within the rules of kube-scheduler. If you are looking for more flexibility, it is wise to choose to run a custom scheduler. Custom schedulers are external applications, so they are not limited to the scheduling framework's flow and requests.

In the following sections, you will learn the details of both methods and see them in action.

Configure and Manage Multiple Schedulers

Kubernetes scheduler assigns pods to nodes with its elaborate architecture and rich configuration capabilities. However, if the default scheduler does not fit your requirements, it is possible to create a new one and run them

149

simultaneously. The basic idea of multiple schedulers is based on a field in pod specification: schedulerName. If the field is specified, the pod is dispatched by the corresponding scheduler. On the other hand, if it is not set, the default scheduler dispatches the pod.

Let's start by creating a multi-node cluster by running minikube start --nodes 5 if you have no cluster up and running. Then, you can create a pod and check it is schedulerName.

Listing 5-5. Pod with the default scheduler

```
$ kubectl run nginx-by-default-scheduler --image=nginx

$ kubectl get pods
NAME                          READY   STATUS    RESTARTS   AGE
nginx-by-default-scheduler    1/1     Running   0          99s

$ kubectl get pods nginx-by-default-scheduler -o jsonpath=
"{.spec.schedulerName}"
default-scheduler
```

When you create without specifying the schedulerName field, it is filled by the default value and then assigned by the default scheduler. Now, let's create another pod to be handled by a custom scheduler.

Listing 5-6. Pod with a custom scheduler

```
$ kubectl run nginx-by-custom-scheduler --image=nginx --overrid
es='{"spec":{"schedulerName":"custom-scheduler"}}'
pod/nginx-by-custom-scheduler created

$ kubectl get pods nginx-by-custom-scheduler
NAME                         READY   STATUS    RESTARTS   AGE
nginx-by-custom-scheduler    0/1     Pending   0          16s
```

The pod is in Pending state because there is no scheduler to handle it. It is now time to deploy a second scheduler to cluster to handle pods with the schedulerName field equals custom-scheduler.

In the custom-scheduler, we will disable all *beta* features that are enabled in the upstream scheduler. The scheduler will run in the kube-system namespace next to the kube-scheduler. Create a file with the name kube-scheduler-custom.yaml with the following content.

Listing 5-7. Custom scheduler pod definition

```yaml
apiVersion: v1
kind: Pod
metadata:
  name: kube-scheduler-custom
  namespace: kube-system
spec:
  containers:
  - name: kube-scheduler-custom
    image: k8s.gcr.io/kube-scheduler:v1.19.0
    command:
    - kube-scheduler
    - --kubeconfig=/etc/kubernetes/scheduler.conf
    - --leader-elect=false
    - --scheduler-name=custom-scheduler
    - --feature-gates=AllBeta=false
    volumeMounts:
    - mountPath: /etc/kubernetes/scheduler.conf
      name: kubeconfig
      readOnly: true
  nodeName: minikube
  restartPolicy: Always
  volumes:
```

```
  - hostPath:
      path: /etc/kubernetes/scheduler.conf
      type: FileOrCreate
    name: kubeconfig
```

The pod is a frank definition to run k8s.gcr.io/kube-scheduler:v1.19.0 image and attaching the kubeconfig as read-only volume. Three of the following flags define the features of the custom scheduler:

- leader-elect=false disables the leader election stage before running the scheduler since only one instance of the custom scheduler will run.

- scheduler-name=custom-scheduler defines the name of the scheduler.

- feature-gates=AllBeta=false disables all beta features.

Create the deployment with kubectl apply -f kube-scheduler-custom.yaml file and check the pod status.

Listing 5-8. Custom scheduler pod in the cluster

```
$  kubectl -n kube-system get pods kube-scheduler-custom
NAME                     READY   STATUS     RESTARTS   AGE
kube-scheduler-custom    1/1     Running    0          24s
```

Now, check the status of our pod, which is stuck in Pending.

Listing 5-9. Pod assignment

```
$ kubectl get pods nginx-by-custom-scheduler
NAME                        READY   STATUS    RESTARTS   AGE
nginx-by-custom-scheduler   1/1     Running   0          42s
```

The pod is in the `Running` stage, and it means that the custom scheduler worked flawlessly. Creating custom schedulers may not be part of every cloud engineer's daily routine because the default Kubernetes scheduler works quite well for most cases. However, when you need to implement more complex requirements, you will create your custom scheduler and deploy it to the cluster. Let's assume you want to create a scheduler for cost minimization. In your custom scheduler, you may need to assign pods to the cheapest nodes first. Instead, you can create a custom scheduler that considers monitoring metrics while choosing a node. In that case, you may need to distribute pods to the nodes to minimize total latency in the system. However, minimizing the cost or optimizing the latency is conditioned on external systems and not in the default Kubernetes scheduler's scope.

Running multiple schedulers and tagging the pods with their desired scheduler are a straightforward Kubernetes-native approach. The vital part is developing a bulletproof scheduler. There are three crucial points to consider while creating and operating a custom scheduler:

- **Kubernetes API Compatibility**: Scheduler interacts with Kubernetes API to watch pods, retrieve the list of nodes, and create bindings. Therefore, you need to develop custom schedulers that are compatible with the Kubernetes API version. If you are using one of the official client libraries, luckily, you only need to use the correct versions.

- **High Availability**: If your scheduler goes down or runs into failure, it will result in pods in the Pending state. Thus, your applications will not run in the cluster. Therefore, you need to design the application to run with high availability.

- **Play Along Well with the Default Scheduler**: If there is more than one decision-maker in the cluster, you need to be careful of conflicting decisions. For instance, the default scheduler controls the resource requests and limits. If your custom scheduler fills the nodes without considering cluster resources, the default scheduler's pods may move to the other nodes. Therefore, your custom scheduler should play nicely with the default one and avoid conflicting decisions.

In the following exercise, you will create a custom scheduler from scratch using kubebuilder. Also, you will run it in the cluster and assign some pods to nodes.

EXERCISE: DEVELOPING A CUSTOM SCHEDULER WITH KUBEBUILDER

In this exercise, you will create a custom *chaos* scheduler using kubebuilder. Essentially, the schedulers are controllers to watch pods in the cluster. Therefore, you will create a controller and implement reconciliation methods. Finally, you will run the controller and see it in action.

Note   The rest of the exercise is based on kubebuilder, and it requires the following prerequisites: kubebuilder v2.3.1, Go version v1.14+, access to a Kubernetes cluster, and kubectl.

---

1. Initialize the project structure with the following commands:

    ```
    $ mkdir -p $GOPATH/src/extend-k8s.io/chaos-scheduler
    $ cd $GOPATH/src/extend-k8s.io/chaos-scheduler
    $ kubebuilder init
    Writing scaffold for you to edit...
    Get controller runtime:
    $ go get sigs.k8s.io/controller-runtime@v0.5.0
    ```

```
Update go.mod:
$ go mod tidy
Running make:
$ make
.../bin/controller-gen object:headerFile="hack/
boilerplate.go.txt" paths="./..."
go fmt ./...
go vet ./...
go build -o bin/manager main.go
Next: define a resource with:
$ kubebuilder create api
```

The commands create a folder and bootstrap the project with boilerplate code.

2. Create controller for watching the pods with the following command:

```
$ kubebuilder create api --kind Pod --group core --version v1
Create Resource [y/n]
n
Create Controller [y/n]
y
Writing scaffold for you to edit...
controllers/pod_controller.go
Running make:
$ make
.../bin/controller-gen object:headerFile="hack/
boilerplate.go.txt" paths="./..."
go fmt ./...
go vet ./...
go build -o bin/manager main.go
```

Since pods are already Kubernetes resources, skip Create Resource prompt by selecting no. However, accept the second prompt to generate a controller for pod resources.

3. Open the pod_controlller.go located at controllers
    folder. You will see two functions SetupWithManager and
    Reconcile. SetupWithManager is the function that is called
    when the controller starts. Reconcile is the function that is
    invoked by every watched change in the cluster.

    Change the SetupWithManager function with the following content:

```go
func (r *PodReconciler) SetupWithManager(mgr ctrl.
Manager) error {

        filter := predicate.Funcs{
            CreateFunc: func(e event.CreateEvent) bool {
                pod, ok := e.Object.(*corev1.Pod)
                if ok {
                    if pod.Spec.SchedulerName ==
                    "chaos-scheduler" && pod.Spec.
                    NodeName == "" {
                        return true
                    }
                    return false
                }
                return false
            },
            UpdateFunc: func(e event.UpdateEvent) bool {
                return false
            },
            DeleteFunc: func(e event.DeleteEvent) bool {
                return false
            },
        }
```

```
return ctrl.NewControllerManagedBy(mgr).
    For(&corev1.Pod{}).
    WithEventFilter(filter).
    Complete(r)
}
```

It adds a filter to watch creation events of pods with the schedulerName `chaos-scheduler` and empty nodeName.

Change the `Reconcile` function with the following content:

```
func (r *PodReconciler) Reconcile(req ctrl.Request)
(ctrl.Result, error) {
    ctx := context.Background()
    log := r.Log.WithValues("pod", req.NamespacedName)

    nodes := new(corev1.NodeList)
    err := r.Client.List(ctx, nodes)
    if err != nil {
        return ctrl.Result{Requeue: true}, err
    }

    node := nodes.Items[rand.Intn(len(nodes.Items))].Name
    log.Info("scheduling", "node", node)

    binding := new(corev1.Binding)
    binding.Name = req.Name
    binding.Namespace = req.Namespace
    binding.Target = corev1.ObjectReference{
        Kind:       "Node",
        APIVersion: "v1",
        Name:       node,
    }
```

```
        err = r.Client.Create(ctx, binding)
        if err != nil {
                return ctrl.Result{Requeue: true}, err
        }

        return ctrl.Result{}, nil
}
```

The updated Reconcile function does the following:

- Retrieve the list of nodes.

- Select a node randomly.

- Create a binding resource including the node and pod.

- Send the binding resource to Kubernetes API.

    Choosing a random node is the essential part of the scheduler to create chaos. It will test the capability and resilience of Kubernetes to turbulent and unexpected conditions.

Note   Chaos engineering is a common approach to experiment with a system under ever-changing situations, namely, chaos. The method experiments large-scale and distributed applications to build confidence in elasticity and resilience.

Add the following libraries to import list of pod_controlller.go:

```
"math/rand"
"sigs.k8s.io/controller-runtime/pkg/event"
"sigs.k8s.io/controller-runtime/pkg/predicate"
```

4. Start the controller with the following command:

```
$ make run
../bin/controller-gen object:headerFile="hack/
boilerplate.go.txt" paths="./..."
```

```
go fmt ./...
go vet ./...
../bin/controller-gen "crd:trivialVersions=true"
rbac:roleName=manager-role webhook paths="./..." output:c
rd:artifacts:config=config/crd/bases
go run ./main.go
INFO      controller-runtime.metrics    metrics server is
starting to listen    {"addr": ":8080"}
INFO      setup            starting manager
INFO      controller-runtime.manager    starting metrics
server           {"path": "/metrics"}
INFO      controller-runtime.controller    Starting
EventSource     {"controller": "pod", "source": "kind
source: /, Kind="}
INFO      controller-runtime.controller    Starting
Controller      {"controller": "pod"}
INFO      controller-runtime.controller    Starting
workers   {"controller": "pod", "worker count": 1}
```

As the logs show, the controller started and waited for the events of pods in the cluster.

5. In another terminal, create a pod to be scheduled by chaos-scheduler:

```
$ kubectl run nginx-by-chaos-scheduler --image=nginx --ov
errides='{"spec":{"schedulerName":"chaos-scheduler"}}'
pod/nginx-by-chaos-scheduler created
```

6. Check the logs of controller started in Step 4:

```
...
INFO      controllers.Pod      scheduling      {"pod":
"default/nginx-by-chaos-scheduler", "node":
"minikube-m02"}
DEBUG     controller-runtime.controller    Successfully
Reconciled    {"controller": "pod", "request": "default/
nginx-by-chaos-scheduler"}
```

The additional log lines indicate that the custom scheduler assigned the pod.

7. Check the status of pod started in Step 5:

```
$ kubectl get pods nginx-by-chaos-scheduler
NAME                        READY  STATUS   RESTARTS  AGE
nginx-by-chaos-scheduler  1/1    Running  0         34s
```

The chaos scheduler assigned the new pod to a node, and it is running. It shows that the custom scheduler developed from scratch using kubebuilder works flawlessly.

In the following section, we will extend the Kubernetes scheduler with the second extension point: scheduler extenders. The scheduler extender approach will work as webhooks and interfere with the scheduling framework stages.

Scheduler Extenders

Scheduler extenders are external webhooks to tweak scheduling decisions in the different phases of the scheduling framework. The framework has multiple stages to find a suitable node, and in each step, it calls plugins compiled into kube-scheduler. In four particular phases, it also calls scheduler extenders: *Filter, Score/Prioritize, Preempt,* and *Bind.* The responses from the webhooks are combined with the results of scheduler plugins. Thus, scheduler extenders facilitate an extension of the kube-scheduler without diving into its source code.

In this section, configuration details and extender API will be covered. In the end, you will develop a scheduler extender webhook server and run it with the Kubernetes cluster.

Configuration Details

Kubernetes scheduler connects to external processes, so it should know where to connect and evaluate responses. The configuration is passed via a file with the schema of KubeSchedulerConfiguration. A minimal configuration looks as follows.

Listing 5-10. Minimal KubeSchedulerConfiguration

```
apiVersion: kubescheduler.config.k8s.io/v1beta1
kind: KubeSchedulerConfiguration
clientConnection:
  kubeconfig: /etc/kubernetes/scheduler.conf
```

Note Comprehensive details of KubeSchedulerConfiguration is available in reference documentation.

You can also add extenders to KubeSchedulerConfiguration as follows.

Listing 5-11. Extenders in KubeSchedulerConfiguration

```
apiVersion: kubescheduler.config.k8s.io/v1beta1
kind: KubeSchedulerConfiguration
clientConnection:
  kubeconfig: /etc/kubernetes/scheduler.conf
extenders:
- urlPrefix: http://localhost:8888/
  filterVerb: filter
  ignorable: true
  weight: 1
- urlPrefix: http://localhost:8890/
  filterVerb: filter
```

```
prioritizeVerb: prioritize
bindVerb: bind
ignorable: false
weight: 1
```

In the preceding example, two extenders are running on `localhost:8888` and `localhost:8890`. The first one is called for filtering nodes only, and when it fails, it will not block the scheduling. However, the second one is called for filtering, scoring, and binding phases of the framework. Besides, it is not ignorable, so if the webhook is not reachable or fails, the pod's scheduling will be stuck at `Pending`.

Note   You can check fields of extender configuration in the source code as it is not part of Kubernetes API documentation.

After configuring the `kube-scheduler` with extender information, now let's dive into the interaction between them.

Scheduler Extender API

Kubernetes scheduler makes HTTP calls to extenders with the data related to its stage and expects structured responses. In your scheduler extender, you need to implement these calls with their JSON request and responses. The essential advantage is that you can develop the extender in any language independent from Kubernetes binaries.

Filter

Filter webhooks receive the following data as argument.

Listing 5-12. ExtenderArgs data structure

```
type ExtenderArgs struct {
    // Pod being scheduled
    Pod *v1.Pod
    // List of candidate nodes where the pod can be
    // scheduled; to be populated only if
    // Extender.NodeCacheCapable == false
    Nodes *v1.NodeList
    // List of candidate node names where the pod
    // can be scheduled; to be populated only if
    // Extender.NodeCacheCapable == true
    NodeNames *[]string
}
```

It simply consists of a pod and a list of nodes or node names based on the cache status in extenders. As a response, the following data structure is sent back.

Listing 5-13. ExtenderFilterResult data structure

```
type ExtenderFilterResult struct {
    // Filtered set of nodes where the pod can be scheduled
    // only if Extender.NodeCacheCapable == false
    Nodes *v1.NodeList
    // Filtered set of nodes where the pod can be scheduled
    // only if Extender.NodeCacheCapable == true
    NodeNames *[]string
    // Filtered out nodes where the pod can't be scheduled
    // and the failure messages
```

```
      FailedNodes FailedNodesMap
      // Error message indicating failure
      Error string
}

type FailedNodesMap map[string]string
```

The response consists of the filtered nodes for the pod. In addition, the unschedulable nodes are sent back as `FailedNodes` with their messages. Finally, there is an `Error` field if the filtering fails for any reason.

Prioritize

Prioritize webhooks receive the same data structure, `ExtenderArgs`, like filter webhooks. The webhook is expected to create scores for the nodes to assign the pod and send back the following data structure.

Listing 5-14. `HostPriorityList` data structure

```
type HostPriorityList []HostPriority

type HostPriority struct {
      // Name of the host
      Host string
      // Score associated with the host
      Score int64
}
```

Scores from the webhook are added to the ones calculated by other extenders and Kubernetes scheduler plugins. The scheduling framework selects the node with the highest score for the pod assignment.

Preempt

When Kubernetes schedules pods to nodes, finding a suitable node in the cluster is not always possible. In that case, preemption logic is triggered to evict some pods from the node. If preemption runs successfully, the pod will be scheduled to the node, and the evicted ones will find a new home. During preemption, the scheduler also calls enabled webhooks with the following data structure.

Listing 5-15. ExtenderPreemptionArgs data structure

```
type ExtenderPreemptionArgs struct {
      //pod being scheduled
      Pod *v1.Pod
      // Victims map generated by scheduler preemption phase
      // Only set NodeNameToMetaVictims if
      // Extender.NodeCacheCapable == true.
      // Otherwise, only set NodeNameToVictims.
      NodeNameToVictims       map[string]*Victims
      NodeNameToMetaVictims map[string]*MetaVictims
}

type Victims struct {
       // a group of pods expected to be preempted.
      Pods               []*v1.Pod
      // the count of violations of PodDisruptionBudget
      NumPDBViolations int64
}

type MetaVictims struct {
       // a group of pods expected to be preempted.
      Pods               []*v1.Pod
      // the count of violations of PodDisruptionBudget
      NumPDBViolations int64
}
```

The data consists of a pod and a map of potential nodes with `Victims` living on these nodes. In response, the webhook sends the following data.

Listing 5-16. `ExtenderPreemptionResult` data structure

```
type ExtenderPreemptionResult struct {
    NodeNameToMetaVictims map[string]*MetaVictims
}
```

The webhook evaluates the nodes and pods for preemption and sends back potential victims.

Bind

Bind call is used to delegate the node and pod assignment. When it is implemented, it becomes the extender's responsibility to interact with Kubernetes API for binding. Webhooks receive the following data as an argument.

Listing 5-17. `ExtenderBindingArgs` data structure

```
type ExtenderBindingArgs struct {
    // PodName is the name of the pod being bound
    PodName string
    // PodNamespace is the namespace of the pod being bound
    PodNamespace string
    // PodUID is the UID of the pod being bound
    PodUID types.UID
    // Node selected by the scheduler
    Node string
}
```

In response, it returns if an error happened during binding.

Listing 5-18. ExtenderBindingResult data structure

```
type ExtenderBindingResult struct {
    // Error message indicating failure
    Error string
}
```

In the following exercise, you will create a scheduler extender from scratch and use it in action. The extender will interfere with scheduling framework decisions and the assignment of pods to nodes.

EXERCISE: DEVELOPING AND RUNNING A SCHEDULER EXTENDER

In this exercise, you will create a custom chaos scheduler extender and run it inside the Kubernetes cluster. You will develop an HTTP web server in Go since scheduler extenders are webhook servers in principle. In addition, you will configure the kube-scheduler in minikube to connect to your scheduler extender.

Note   The rest of the exercise is based on writing a web server in Go, and it requires the following prerequisites: Docker, minikube, and kubectl.

---

1. Start a multi-node cluster in minikube with the following command:

    ```
    $ minikube start --kubernetes-version v1.19.0 --nodes 5
    ```

2. Create the following folder structure in your Go environment:

    ```
    $ mkdir -p cd $GOPATH/src/extend-k8s.io/k8s-scheduler-
    extender
    $ cd $GOPATH/src/extend-k8s.io/k8s-scheduler-extender
    $ mkdir -p cmd manifests pkg/filter pkg/prioritize
    $ tree -a
    ```

```
.
├── cmd
├── manifests
└── pkg
    ├── filter
    └── prioritize
```

`5 directories, 0 files`

The folder structure is the mainstream way of creating a Go application. In the following steps, you will create files in each directory.

3. Create a file `flip.go` in `pkg/filter` folder with the following content:

```
package filter

import (
        "math/rand"
        "time"

        "github.com/sirupsen/logrus"
)

const (
        HEADS = "heads"
        TAILS = "tails"
)

var coin []string

func init() {
        rand.Seed(time.Now().UnixNano())
        coin = []string{HEADS, TAILS}
}
```

```go
func Flip() string {

        side := coin[rand.Intn(len(coin))]
        logrus.Info("Flipped the coin and it is ", side)
        return side
}
```

The function Flip returns either heads or tails to filter the nodes randomly.

Create a file filter.go in pkg/filter folder with the following content:

```go
package filter

import (
        "fmt"

        corev1 "k8s.io/api/core/v1"
        extenderv1 "k8s.io/kube-scheduler/extender/v1"
)

func Filter(args extenderv1.ExtenderArgs) extenderv1.
ExtenderFilterResult {

        filtered := make([]corev1.Node, 0)
        failed := make(extenderv1.FailedNodesMap)

        pod := args.Pod

        for _, node := range args.Nodes.Items {

                side := Flip()
                if side == HEADS {
                        filtered = append(filtered, node)
                } else {
```

```
                    failed[node.Name] = fmt.Sprintf("%s
                    cannot be scheduled to %s: coin is %s",
                    pod.Name, node.Name, side)
            }
        }

        return extenderv1.ExtenderFilterResult{
                Nodes: &corev1.NodeList{
                        Items: filtered,
                },
                FailedNodes: failed,
        }

}
```

The Filter function implements the logic of the scheduler extender call by receiving ExtenderArgs as an argument and ExtenderFilterResult as a response.

4. Create a file roll.go in pkg/prioritize folder with the following content:

```
package prioritize

import (
        "math/rand"
        "time"

        "github.com/sirupsen/logrus"
        extenderv1 "k8s.io/kube-scheduler/extender/v1"
)

func init() {
        rand.Seed(time.Now().UnixNano())
}
```

```
func Roll() int64 {

    number := rand.Int63n(extenderv1.
    MaxExtenderPriority + 1)
    logrus.Info("Rolled the dice and it is ", number)

    return number

}
```

Roll function imitates rolling dice to find a score for the nodes. Create a file prioritize.go in pkg/prioritize folder with the following content:

```
package prioritize

import (
    extenderv1 "k8s.io/kube-scheduler/extender/v1"
)

func Prioritize(args extenderv1.ExtenderArgs) extenderv1.
HostPriorityList {

    hostPriority := make(extenderv1.HostPriorityList, 0)

    for _, node := range args.Nodes.Items {
        hostPriority = append(hostPriority,
        extenderv1.HostPriority{
            Host:  node.Name,
            Score: Roll(),
        })
    }

    return hostPriority

}
```

Prioritize function implements the scheduler extender call to receive ExtenderArgs and send HostPriorityList back to kube-scheduler.

5. Create a main.go file under cmd folder with the following content:

```
package main

import (
        "encoding/json"
        "log"
        "net/http"

        "github.com/gorilla/mux"
        "github.com/extend-k8s.io/k8s-scheduler-extender/
        pkg/filter"
        "github.com/extend-k8s.io/k8s-scheduler-extender/
        pkg/prioritize"
        "github.com/sirupsen/logrus"

        extenderv1 "k8s.io/kube-scheduler/extender/v1"
)

func main() {
        r := mux.NewRouter()

        r.HandleFunc("/", homeHandler)
        r.HandleFunc("/filter", filterHandler)
        r.HandleFunc("/prioritize", prioritizeHandler)

        log.Fatal(http.ListenAndServe(":8888", r))
}

func filterHandler(w http.ResponseWriter, r *http.
Request) {

        args := extenderv1.ExtenderArgs{}
        response := extenderv1.ExtenderFilterResult{}

        if err := json.NewDecoder(r.Body).Decode(&args);
        err != nil {
                response.Error = err.Error()
```

```
    } else {
        response = filter.Filter(args)
    }

    w.Header().Set("Content-Type", "application/json")
    if err := json.NewEncoder(w).Encode(response); err
    != nil {
        logrus.Error(err)
        return
    }

}

func prioritizeHandler(w http.ResponseWriter, r *http.
Request) {

    args := extenderv1.ExtenderArgs{}
    response := make(extenderv1.HostPriorityList, 0)

    if err := json.NewDecoder(r.Body).Decode(&args);
    err == nil {
        response = prioritize.Prioritize(args)
    }

    w.Header().Set("Content-Type", "application/json")
    if err := json.NewEncoder(w).Encode(response);
    err != nil {
        logrus.Error(err)
        return
    }
}

func homeHandler(w http.ResponseWriter, r *http.Request)
{

    w.Write([]byte("scheduler extender is running!"))
}
```

It is the entry point of the webhook server with HTTP handlers for filter and prioritize calls. The server will run on the 8888 port by default.

6. Create a go.mod file in the root folder to set the dependency versions:

```
module github.com/extend-k8s.io/k8s-scheduler-extender

go 1.14

require (
        github.com/gorilla/mux v1.8.0
        github.com/sirupsen/logrus v1.6.0
        k8s.io/api v0.19.0
        k8s.io/kube-scheduler v0.19.0
)
```

7. Create a Dockerfile in the root folder to build container images in the following steps:

```
FROM golang:1.14-alpine as builder
ADD . /go/src/github.com/extend-k8s.io/k8s-scheduler-
extender
WORKDIR /go/src/github.com/extend-k8s.io/k8s-scheduler-
extender/cmd
RUN go build -v

FROM alpine:latest
COPY --from=builder /go/src/github.com/extend-k8s.io/k8s-
scheduler-extender/cmd/cmd /usr/local/bin/k8s-scheduler-
extender
CMD ["k8s-scheduler-extender"]
```

8. Now, you can build and push the Docker image of your scheduler extender with the following commands:

Note   Set DOCKER_REPOSITORY environment variable according to your Docker repository.

```
$ docker build -t $DOCKER_REPOSITORY/k8s-scheduler-
extender:v1 .
Step 1/7 : FROM golang:1.14-alpine as builder
...
Step 7/7 : CMD ["k8s-scheduler-extender"]
 ---> Running in 6655404206c1
Removing intermediate container 6655404206c1
 ---> 0ce4bb201541
Successfully built 0ce4bb201541
Successfully tagged $DOCKER_REPOSITORY/k8s-scheduler-
extender:v1

$ docker push $DOCKER_REPOSITORY/k8s-scheduler-
extender:v1
The push refers to repository [docker.io/$DOCKER_
REPOSITORY/k8s-scheduler-extender]
...
v1: digest: sha256:0e62a24a4b9e9e0215f5f02e37b5f86d9235ee
950e740069f80951e370ae5b34 size: 739
```

9. Create a Kubernetes scheduler configuration file with the name kube-scheduler-config.yaml under manifests folder:

```
apiVersion: kubescheduler.config.k8s.io/v1beta1
kind: KubeSchedulerConfiguration
clientConnection:
  kubeconfig: /etc/kubernetes/scheduler.conf
extenders:
```

```
- urlPrefix: http://localhost:8888/
  filterVerb: filter
  prioritizeVerb: prioritize
  weight: 1
```

It is a simple configuration that will be passed to the kube-scheduler, and it defines the location of your extender with endpoints.

10. Create a Kubernetes scheduler pod file to replace the default pod definition of kube-scheduler. Set the filename kube-scheduler.yaml under manifests folder with the following content:

```
apiVersion: v1
kind: Pod
metadata:
  creationTimestamp: null
  labels:
    component: kube-scheduler
    tier: control-plane
  name: kube-scheduler
  namespace: kube-system
spec:
  containers:
  - command:
    - kube-scheduler
    - --authentication-kubeconfig=/etc/kubernetes/
      scheduler.conf
    - --authorization-kubeconfig=/etc/kubernetes/
      scheduler.conf
    - --bind-address=127.0.0.1
    - --kubeconfig=/etc/kubernetes/scheduler.conf
    - --leader-elect=false
    - --port=0
```

```
- --config=/etc/kubernetes/kube-scheduler-config.yaml
image: k8s.gcr.io/kube-scheduler:v1.19.0
imagePullPolicy: IfNotPresent
livenessProbe:
  failureThreshold: 8
  httpGet:
    host: 127.0.0.1
    path: /healthz
    port: 10259
    scheme: HTTPS
  initialDelaySeconds: 10
  periodSeconds: 10
  timeoutSeconds: 15
name: kube-scheduler
resources:
  requests:
    cpu: 100m
startupProbe:
  failureThreshold: 24
  httpGet:
    host: 127.0.0.1
    path: /healthz
    port: 10259
    scheme: HTTPS
  initialDelaySeconds: 10
  periodSeconds: 10
  timeoutSeconds: 15
volumeMounts:
- mountPath: /etc/kubernetes/scheduler.conf
  name: kubeconfig
  readOnly: true
- mountPath: /etc/kubernetes/kube-scheduler-config.
  yaml
  name: kube-scheduler-config
```

```
        readOnly: true
    hostNetwork: true
    priorityClassName: system-node-critical
    volumes:
    - hostPath:
        path: /etc/kubernetes/scheduler.conf
        type: FileOrCreate
      name: kubeconfig
    - hostPath:
        path: /etc/kubernetes/kube-scheduler-config.yaml
        type: FileOrCreate
      name: kube-scheduler-config
status: {}
```

It adds three sections to use the kube-scheduler-config.yaml from Step 9.

- A command flag config

- A volume with the name kube-scheduler-config

- A volume mount for the volume kube-scheduler-config

11. Create a pod definition for scheduler extender with the name kube-scheduler-extender.yaml under manifests folder with the following content:

```
apiVersion: v1
kind: Pod
metadata:
  labels:
    component: kube-scheduler-extender
    tier: control-plane
  name: kube-scheduler-extender
  namespace: kube-system
```

```
spec:
  containers:
  - image: DOCKER_REPOSITORY/k8s-scheduler-extender:v1
    name: kube-scheduler-extender
  hostNetwork: true
```

Note   Do not forget to change DOCKER_REPOSITORY to the environment variable set in Step 8.

---

12. Mount the current working directory into minikube node with the following command:

```
$ minikube mount $(pwd):/etc/k8s-scheduler-extender
```
📁   Mounting host path .../src/extend-k8s.io/k8s-scheduler
      -extender into VM as /etc/k8s-scheduler-extender ...

      ...

🚀   Userspace file server: ufs starting
✅   Successfully mounted .../src/extend-k8s.io/k8s-
      scheduler-extender to /etc/k8s-scheduler-extender

💫   NOTE: This process must stay alive for the mount to
      be accessible ...

13. In another terminal, SSH into the minikube node and copy the manifests with the following commands, and restart the kubelet:

```
$ minikube ssh
docker@minikube:~$ sudo su

root@minikube:/home/docker# cp /etc/k8s-scheduler-
extender/manifests/kube-scheduler-extender.yaml /etc/
kubernetes/manifests/kube-scheduler-extender.yaml

root@minikube:/home/docker# cp /etc/k8s-scheduler-
extender/manifests/kube-scheduler-config.yaml /etc/
kubernetes/kube-scheduler-config.yaml
```

```
root@minikube:/home/docker# cp /etc/k8s-scheduler-
extender/manifests/kube-scheduler.yaml /etc/kubernetes/
manifests/kube-scheduler.yaml

root@minikube:/home/docker# systemctl restart kubelet
```

In the copy steps, you have added manifests and configuration files to the locations where kubelet looks for. In the last step, you have restarted the kubelet to load the new files and work with them. You can exit from the minikube node and continue on your local workstation.

14. Create a deployment with 25 replicas and watch for the events in the cluster:

```
$ kubectl create deployment nginx --image=nginx
--replicas=25
deployment.apps/nginx created
$  kubectl get events --field-selector
reason=FailedScheduling
LAST SEEN    TYPE       REASON              OBJECT
MESSAGE
...
3m23s       Warning   FailedScheduling    pod/nginx-
6799fc88d8-qnn9p   0/5 nodes are available: 1 nginx-
6799fc88d8-qnn9p cannot be scheduled to minikube-m02:
coin is tails, 1 nginx-6799fc88d8-qnn9p cannot be
scheduled to minikube-m03: coin is tails, 1 nginx-
6799fc88d8-qnn9p cannot be scheduled to minikube-m04:
coin is tails, 1 nginx-6799fc88d8-qnn9p cannot be
scheduled to minikube-m05: coin is tails, 1 nginx-
6799fc88d8-qnn9p cannot be scheduled to minikube: coin is
tails.
...
```

If you are lucky and get tails for all five nodes, the pod will have similar events. If you are not lucky to see the event, you can also check the logs of the scheduler extender:

```
$ kubectl -n kube-system logs -f kube-scheduler-extender-
minikube
...
time=".." level=info msg="Flipped the coin and it is
heads"
time=".." level=info msg="Flipped the coin and it is
heads"
time=".." level=info msg="Flipped the coin and it is
tails"
time=".." level=info msg="Flipped the coin and it is
heads"
time=".." level=info msg="Flipped the coin and it is
tails"
time=".." level=info msg="Rolled the dice and it is 1"
time=".." level=info msg="Rolled the dice and it is 10"
time=".." level=info msg="Rolled the dice and it is 1"
...
```

It shows that the kube-scheduler is configured correctly, and it connects to the scheduler extender webhook. The webhook filters the nodes randomly by flipping the coin. In addition, it scores the nodes by rolling the dice. In other words, the scheduler extender generates some randomness and chaos into the scheduling process.

Developing and running scheduler extenders is straightforward since you can extend the existing default scheduler's functionality without recompiling the binary. Also, you can create the extender in any programming language you want. However, it would be best if you were careful on the following issues since you generate a touchpoint to Kubernetes control plane component:

- **Configuration**: Extenders are defined with a static file to the Kubernetes scheduler. Therefore, ensure that the file location and its content are correct. In addition, ensure that the file will not be overwritten or deleted with the cluster upgrades.

- **Performance**: Like all webhooks, extenders run as external processes. Connecting to another server and retrieving the response are costly in terms of time. Ensure that the webhook is providing responses as fast as possible and it is reachable by the control plane components.

- **Cache Inconsistency**: It is possible to enable caches in extenders for node information. If your nodes do not change often or scheduling decisions are not so critical, it would be beneficial to cache the node information in extenders. On the other hand, if you always need the recent information about the nodes, disable the caches and work with the data sent to you by the Kubernetes scheduler.

Key Takeaways

- Kubernetes scheduler is the control plane component to assign workload over the cluster.

- Kubernetes scheduler chooses the best possible node within the priorities and rules set.

- It is possible to extend scheduling decisions by running multiple schedulers in the cluster.

- The scheduling framework is the pluggable architecture of the Kubernetes scheduler, and it is extendible by webhooks.

In the following chapter, we will extend the interaction of Kubernetes with the infrastructure by developing and running storage, networking, and device plugins.

CHAPTER 6

Infrastructure Extensions

Move fast with stable infrastructure.

> —Mark Zuckerberg
> American entrepreneur and
> founder and CEO of Facebook

Kubernetes is the de facto container orchestration system for what it offers and also what it does not offer. Kubernetes comes with scalable and reliable container runtime management, but it leaves infrastructure-related decisions to the end users. It allows users to create their clusters on any infrastructure as long as it is compliant with APIs. This chapter will focus on extending the Kubernetes by changing the underlying cloud-native infrastructure. At the end of this chapter, you will configure and run storage, networking, and device plugins that implement custom and flexible requirements.

Let's start with an overview of the cloud-native infrastructure and how Kubernetes integrates it.

© Onur Yilmaz 2021
O. Yilmaz, *Extending Kubernetes*, https://doi.org/10.1007/978-1-4842-7095-0_6

Cloud-Native Infrastructure

Kubernetes is not a *"Write once, run anywhere"* type of system, but it also does not restrict any cloud provider or on-prem system. It allows users to choose from a wide range of open infrastructure options in the ecosystem. You can create a Kubernetes cluster on almost every public cloud provider, inside your datacenter, or even on your laptop. However, making cloud-native applications requires an underlying cloud-native infrastructure. The infrastructure should be designed to take advantage of virtualized and distributed microservice architecture.

Kubernetes is the container orchestration, so its focus is creating, running, and operating containers. However, containers are not simple applications running on bare metal nodes. Instead, they are virtualized systems requiring complicated storage, networking, and device operations. The stack of Kubernetes can be illustrated in Figure 6-1. There are storage, network, and device plugins that interact with the physical infrastructure at the bottom. When it achieves connectivity and volumes, Kubernetes can create and run your containers as the building block of pods. The upper layers of Kubernetes make it possible to develop scalable, reliable, and cloud-native applications with more complex Kubernetes resources.

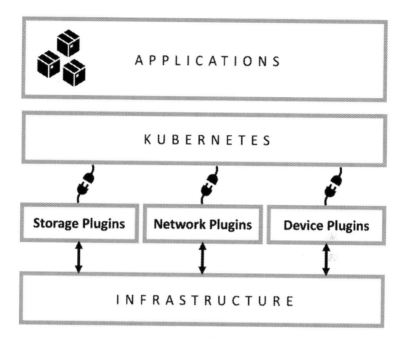

Figure 6-1. *Kubernetes and infrastructure*

The plugins between the infrastructure and Kubernetes are the tools to connect your infrastructures with a custom storage or networking solution. Since Kubernetes does not enforce a "*one size fits all*" approach, it works with every infrastructure provided as long as they are compliant with the publicly available plugin APIs. In the following sections, we will cover the three plugins with their APIs and examples.

Storage Plugins

Storage is one of the challenges in cloud-native architecture with its durability and rigidity characteristics. Containers are temporary, and Kubernetes can restart or reschedule them. If there are volumes attached to the containers, it is possible to lose them too. However, you need to deploy databases, ERP systems, and data-centric applications to Kubernetes, so not all applications running in the cluster are fully ephemeral. Thus, infrastructure should endure the container's application data as a part of *persistent* storage.

Let's see how persistent storage works in Kubernetes. Create a PersistentVolumeClaim (PVC) with the following data.

Listing 6-1. Example PVC

```
kind: PersistentVolumeClaim
apiVersion: v1
metadata:
 name: pvc-test
spec:
 accessModes:
 - ReadWriteOnce
 requests:
 storage: 1Gi
```

Now, check the PersistentVolumeClaim and PersistentVolume resources in the cluster.

Listing 6-2. Volume listing

```
$ kubectl get pvc
NAME        STATUS    VOLUME
CAPACITY    ACCESS MODES    STORAGECLASS    AGE
pvc-test    Bound     pvc-467fa613-0396-481a-aa73-
d4b6c5fbcc4b    1Gi         RWO             standard        10s

$ kubectl get pv
NAME                                    CAPACITY    ACCESS
MODES    RECLAIM POLICY    STATUS    CLAIM
STORAGECLASS    REASON    AGE
```

```
pvc-467fa613-0396-481a-aa73-d4b6c5fbcc4b   1Gi
RWO            Delete          Bound     default/pvc-
test    standard                13s
```

In the PVC, you have requested a volume with 1Gi, and the cluster created one PersistentVolume accordingly. You can now use it in pods, statefulsets, or even functions to store your application data. It seems straightforward with a PVC and PV in Kubernetes because it creates a powerful abstraction from the infrastructure layer. As the end user, we do not need to know the lifecycle of storage in the infrastructure:

- How is the volume created?

- How much capacity is allocated?

- Where is the volume attached?

- How is the access to storage provided?

- How the backup and restore of the volumes are managed?

Communication between storage vendors and Kubernetes is standardized as an open source API. Thus, implementation details and answers to the questions are left to the storage providers. The abstraction between Kubernetes and storage infrastructure is defined in *Container Storage Interface (CSI)*, and you will learn its basics next.

Container Storage Interface (CSI)

Container Storage Interface (CSI) is an open source API to enable container orchestrators to work with storage systems. In the early stages of Kubernetes, volumes are managed by plugins compiled into Kubernetes binaries. As the number of vendors increases, it becomes more complex to manage in-tree plugins. In addition, it creates a closed environment since adding a new storage vendor requires to be a part of Kubernetes source code. On the other hand, CSI plugins are external applications with an open standard API.

From the vendor's point of view, the main advantage is to only develop plugins and follow the CSI requirements. It is enough to work with every container orchestrator such as Kubernetes, Apache Mesos, and many to follow in the future. CSI plugins provide the following capabilities:

- Dynamic provisioning and decommission of volumes

- Attachment/mounting and detachment/unmounting of volumes

The complete specification is available at GitHub with all functions, requests, and responses. The communication between the CSI plugins and container orchestrators is handled by *gRPC (Remote Procedure Call)*, which is an open framework for high-performance communication.

The CSI plugins are divided into two as Node Plugin and Controller Plugin:

- **Node Plugin** is a gRPC server that runs on the node where the storage provider volumes are provisioned.

- **Controller Plugin** is a gRPC server that can run anywhere in the cluster.

The two plugins also implement an Identity gRPC service to provide information about their capabilities. Therefore, you can deploy Node and Controller Plugins as two binaries or can be combined into a single binary.

The lifecycle of a volume with the gRPC calls can be summarized in the following diagram in Figure 6-2.

Figure 6-2. *Lifecycle of a dynamic volume*

The flow starts with a CreateVolume call to *Controller Plugin* to provision a new volume. Then, ControllerPublishVolume call is made to indicate that the container orchestrator wants to use the node on the volume. In this step, the plugin performs the work that is necessary for making the volume available on the given node. Following that, the NodePublishVolume call is sent to *Node Plugin* running on the specific node to publish that a workload is scheduled and it wants to use the volume. Similarly, NodeUnpublishVolume, ControllerUnpublishVolume, and DeleteVolume calls are made while deleting a volume in the storage provider.

CSI interface is straightforward to work with, but engaging volumes into a container orchestration system such as Kubernetes is not so frank. In the following section, you will learn how CSI plugins are integrated into Kubernetes.

CSI Plugins in Kubernetes

CSI is a standard for storage systems to work with container orchestration systems such as Kubernetes. The main idea is for vendors to develop plugins and install them into the container orchestrators. In this section, you will learn how Kubernetes integrates CSI plugins with native Kubernetes resources.

Kubernetes defines the communication between `kubelet` and CSI plugin with the following two rules:

- `kubelet` runs on the node and directly calls CSI functions. Therefore, the CSI plugins should run on the node with their Unix socket available to `kubelet`.

- `kubelet` *finds* the CSI plugins with a plugin registration mechanism. Therefore, CSI plugins should register themselves to the `kubelet` running on the node.

In addition, the Kubernetes storage community provides sidecar containers and resources to minimize deployment effort and boilerplate code. Sidecar containers have the common logic to watch Kubernetes API and trigger actions against CSI plugins. The idea is to bundle sidecar containers with the CSI plugins and deploy them as pods to the cluster. It is not mandatory to use sidecar containers; however, it is highly recommended since they create a powerful abstraction between Kubernetes and CSI. Currently, the following sidecars are maintained:

- **external-provisioner**: It watches for `PersistentVolumeClaim` objects in Kubernetes API and calls `CreateVolume` against the CSI plugin. When the new volume is provisioned, the external-provisioner creates a `PersistentVolume` object in Kubernetes API.

- **external-attacher**: It attaches the volumes to the nodes by calling the `ControllerPublish` function of CSI drivers.

- **external-snapshotter**: It watches for `VolumeSnapshotContent` resources in Kubernetes API and takes `CreateSnapshot`, `DeleteSnapshot`, and `ListSnapshots` actions against CSI driver.

- **external-resizer**: It watches for the changes on
  PersistentVolumeClaim objects to catch if more
  storage is requested. In that case, it calls the
  ControllerExpandVolume function of the CSI plugin.

- **node-driver-registrar**: It fetches CSI driver
  information from the plugin endpoint and registers it
  with the kubelet.

- **livenessprobe**: It monitors the CSI plugin endpoints'
  health and helps Kubernetes restart the pod if necessary.

CSI plugins are typically deployed to Kubernetes as two components
packed by sidecar containers as diagrammed in Figure 6-3.

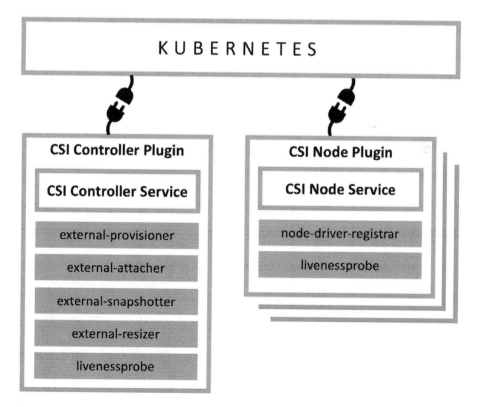

Figure 6-3. *CSI deployment in Kubernetes*

Controller Plugin consists of the CSI plugin that implements controller service and the following sidecars: external-provisioner, external-attacher, external-snapshotter, and external-resizer. It can be deployed as a deployment or statefulset since it can run on any node in the cluster.

Node Plugin consists of a CSI plugin that implements node service with node-driver-registrar sidecar. It should be deployed on every node in the cluster by a DaemonSet.

The sidecars make developing a custom storage plugin, and integrating it into Kubernetes is straightforward. You only need to implement the CSI services following the standard. All cloud providers (such as Google Cloud, Azure, AWS, or AliCloud), infrastructure providers (such as IBM, Dell, VMware, or Hewlett Packard), and storage technologies (such as OpenEBS, GlusterFS, or Vault) have already their CSI drivers ready and publicly available. The following section will configure and deploy a CSI driver to a Kubernetes cluster and see it in action.

CSI Hostpath Driver in Action

CSI Hostpath Driver is a CSI implementation to create volumes using a local directory. Therefore, it is a non-production driver and runs on a single node. In this section, we will deploy it to the cluster and see it in action.

Let's start by creating a minikube cluster by running minikube start --kubernetes-version v1.19.0.

When your cluster is up and running, enable volumesnapshots and csi-hostpath-driver addons.

Listing 6-3. Minikube addons

```
$ minikube addons enable volumesnapshots
✹  The 'volumesnapshots' addon is enabled
$ minikube addons enable csi-hostpath-driver
🔎  Verifying csi-hostpath-driver addon...
✹  The 'csi-hostpath-driver' addon is enabled
```

The first command enables volumesnapshots and deploys the Volume Snapshot Controller along with the volume snapshot CRDs. Since minikube is a single-node cluster, by default, there is no CSI implementation available. The second command deploys *CSI Hostpath Driver*, which will provide storage for you.

The next step is to check which CSIDrivers are installed in the cluster.

Listing 6-4. CSIDrivers in the cluster

```
$ kubectl get CSIDrivers
NAME                    ATTACHREQUIRED    PODINFOONMOUNT
MODES                   AGE
hostpath.csi.k8s.io     true              true
Persistent,Ephemeral    9m17s
```

The name of the CSI drivers follows the domain name notation as hostpath.csi.k8s.io. In addition, there should be StorageClass for volumes managed by the hostpath driver.

Listing 6-5. Storage classes in the cluster

```
$ kubectl get StorageClass
NAME                    PROVISIONER               RECLAIMPOLICY
VOLUMEBINDINGMODE       ALLOWVOLUMEEXPANSION      AGE
csi-hostpath-sc         hostpath.csi.k8s.io       Delete
Immediate               false                     12m
standard (default)      k8s.io/minikube-hostpath  Delete
Immediate               false                     18m
```

In addition to the default storage cluster of minikube, you will see a CSI-managed storage class named csi-hostpath-sc.

Now, let's deep dive into how the plugins and sidecar containers are deployed.

Listing 6-6. Statefulsets in the kube-system namespace

```
$ kubectl -n kube-system get statefulset
NAME                         READY   AGE
csi-hostpath-attacher        1/1     20m
csi-hostpath-provisioner     1/1     20m
csi-hostpath-resizer         1/1     20m
csi-hostpath-snapshotter     1/1     20m
csi-hostpathplugin           1/1     20m
volume-snapshot-controller   1/1     20m
```

You can go over each statefulset one by one and check the containers or run the following jq magic.

Listing 6-7. Statefulsets and containers in the kube-system namespace

```
$ kubectl -n kube-system get statefulsets -o json | jq
'.items[] | "\(.metadata.name): \(.spec.template.spec.
containers[].name)"'
"csi-hostpath-attacher: csi-attacher"
"csi-hostpath-provisioner: csi-provisioner"
"csi-hostpath-resizer: csi-resizer"
"csi-hostpath-snapshotter: csi-snapshotter"
"csi-hostpathplugin: node-driver-registrar"
"csi-hostpathplugin: hostpath"
"csi-hostpathplugin: liveness-probe"
"volume-snapshot-controller: volume-snapshot-controller"
```

As you can see, controller sidecars are running independently, while the node sidecars are packed in the csi-hostpathplugin statefulset. The connection between the sidecars and drivers is handled by sharing Unix sockets as volumes.

Listing 6-8. Description of csi-hostpath-provisioner

```
$ kubectl -n kube-system describe statefulsets csi-hostpath-
provisioner
Name:                    csi-hostpath-provisioner
Namespace:               kube-system
...
  Volumes:
   socket-dir:
    Type:                HostPath (bare host directory volume)
    Path:                /var/lib/kubelet/plugins/csi-hostpath
    HostPathType:  Director
```

As you can see from the previous command output, the csi-provisioner sidecar container connects to the CSI service using the socket defined in the Volume socket-dir.

Create a file named example-pvc.yaml with the following content.

Listing 6-9. Example PVC

```
apiVersion: v1
kind: PersistentVolumeClaim
metadata:
  name: example-pvc
spec:
  accessModes:
  - ReadWriteOnce
  resources:
    requests:
      storage: 1Gi
  storageClassName: csi-hostpath-sc
```

Deploy to the cluster and check the volumes.

Listing 6-10. Volume creation

```
$ kubectl apply -f example-pvc.yaml
persistentvolumeclaim/example-pvc created

$ kubectl get pv
NAME                                          CAPACITY   ACCESS
MODES    RECLAIM POLICY    STATUS    CLAIM
STORAGECLASS         REASON    AGE
pvc-dd4570bc-58cc-4074-a284-b13651970d17    1Gi
RWO              Delete          Bound    default/example-
pvc   csi-hostpath-sc          13s
```

A volume for the PersistentVolumeClaim is created with the correct storage class and it is bound. Let's check the logs of CSI service and check for CreateVolume calls.

Listing 6-11. CSI logs

```
$ kubectl -n kube-system logs csi-hostpathplugin-0 hostpath |
grep -A 3 CreateVolume
* GRPC call: /csi.v1.Controller/CreateVolume
* GRPC request: {"accessibility_requirements":{"prefer
red":[{"segments":{"topology.hostpath.csi/node":"minik
ube"}}],"requisite":[{"segments":{"topology.hostpath.
csi/node":"minikube"}}]},"capacity_range":{"required_
bytes":1073741824},"name":"pvc-dd4570bc-58cc-4074-a284-
b13651970d17","volume_capabilities":[{"AccessType":{"Mount":{}}
,"access_mode":{"mode":1}}]}
created volume af5c51ee-7aa2-11eb-a960-0242ac110004 at path /
csi-data-dir/af5c51ee-7aa2-11eb-a960-0242ac110004
* GRPC response: {"volume":{"accessible_topology":[{"segmen
ts":{"topology.hostpath.csi/node":"minikube"}}],"capacity_
bytes":1073741824,"volume_id":"af5c51ee-7aa2-11eb-a960-
0242ac110004"}}
```

gRPC calls and responses show that the hostpath service created the volume as requested in the `PersistentVolumeClaim`. Sidecar containers handle the conversion from `PersistentVolumeClaim` to a valid CSI call. The abstraction enables that CSI plugins are not concerned about the container orchestrator implementation details.

By following the steps in this section, you have deployed a CSI plugin to a Kubernetes cluster and checked how it is integrated into the Kubernetes ecosystem. In addition, you have seen how it is provisioning storage when requested in Kubernetes. There are three essential points while creating and operating CSI plugins in Kubernetes:

- **CSI Specification and Capabilities**: Ensure that you have implemented all required capabilities concerning your infrastructure.

- **Idempotent and Fault-Tolerant Drivers**: CSI drivers create a bridge between container orchestrators and infrastructure. Therefore, the requests should be idempotent and capable of recovering from failures.

- **Kubernetes Sidecars and Resources**: Kubernetes storage community provides sidecar containers and custom resources to integrate CSI services to the clusters easily. Utilize them as they are maintained for upcoming CSI and Kubernetes versions.

Container Storage Interface (CSI) is the open source API to extend Kubernetes storage operations. It enables working with custom storage requirements and infrastructure characteristics. You can create CSI plugins by implementing the required services and deploy using native Kubernetes resources. Then, you can dynamically create volumes in Kubernetes, and CSI plugins will provision the storage in the infrastructure layer. The abstraction and separation of the concerns make it possible to easily develop, test, and deploy storage extensions to Kubernetes.

The next section will cover the interaction between Kubernetes and networking infrastructure with the Kubernetes networking model and Container Network Interface (CNI) plugins.

Network Plugins

Kubernetes is a scalable container orchestration tool with distributing the workload among multiple nodes in the cluster. Hence, the communication between containers and nodes distributed over the datacenters creates an infrastructure challenge. With its open architecture, Kubernetes does not dictate any networking setting but only defines the requirements. The decoupling of Kubernetes and infrastructure enables vendors to develop their plugins and integrate them into Kubernetes.

In this section, you will learn more about the Kubernetes networking model and the specification for network integrations and, finally, see the plugins in action.

Kubernetes Network Model

The building block of Kubernetes is pods, and every pod gets a unique IP address. This approach creates two significant advantages; firstly, you do not need to develop complex links between pods, including container port to host port matching. Secondly, you can treat pods like VMs in naming, service discovery, load balancing, and application configuration.

Kubernetes requires the following fundamental rules in the networking implementations:

- Pod on a node can communicate with all pods in the cluster without NAT.

- Node agents such as system daemons or kubelet can communicate with all the pods on the same node.

The simplistic model defined with the two rules originates from the VMs with assigned IPs and their communication to other VMs. The model in Kubernetes is named "*IP-per-pod*" which indicates that IP addresses exist at the pod scope. Although implementation details are left to the networking plugins, the three main communication challenges can be discussed and illustrated:

- Containers of the same pod

- Pods on the same node

- Pods on different nodes

A pod in Kubernetes consists of one or more user-defined containers and an additional pause container. You can check the pause containers by connecting to a Kubernetes node.

Listing 6-12. Containers on a Kubernetes node

```
$ docker ps
CONTAINER ID IMAGE COMMAND ...
...
tm574dmcbc gcr.io/google_containers/pause-amd64:3.0 "/pause" ...
...
zsxqd5lcvx gcr.io/google_containers/pause-amd64:3.0 "/pause" ...
...
```

The fundamental task of pause containers is to create and keep the network namespace if other containers crash and reconnect. It ensures that all the pod's containers share a single network namespace and connect via localhost. As diagrammed in Figure 6-4, container A can connect to port 8080 of container B using localhost:8080.

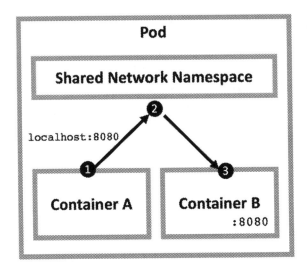

Figure 6-4. *Container to container communication*

Each pod has its network namespace and unique IP address. In addition, each pod has a virtual Ethernet device. The virtual Ethernet devices create a tunnel between the node and the pod's network. The naming of the virtual tunnel is eth0 on the pod side and veth0, veth1, and vethN on the node side. Thus, a request starts from the eth0 interface of the pod and arrives at the vethN interface. On the node, there is a network bridge called cbr0 to connect multiple networks. Every pod on the node is part of the cbr0 bridge, and requests find their way through it, as diagrammed in Figure 6-5.

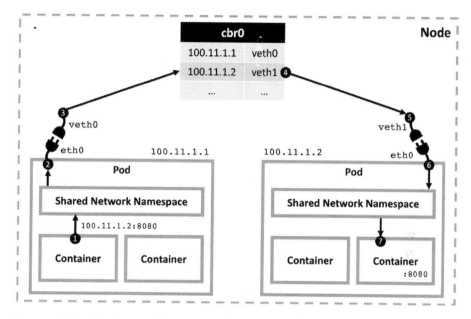

Figure 6-5. *Pod to pod communication on the same node*

Network bridges on the nodes know the pod IPs and their virtual Ethernet devices. When a pod tries to connect to an IP not listed in the network bridge, the routing becomes a little complicated. Although implementation can vary based on networking plugin and infrastructure, we can discuss the request's typical flow as diagrammed in Figure 6-6. When the bridge has no information about the IP, it asks for a default gateway at the cluster level. At the cluster level, an IP table is kept for nodes and their IPs. In a typical setup, pod IPs are allocated between the nodes—for instance, *Node 1* with 100.11.1.0/24 range, *Node 2* with 100.11.2.0/24 range, and so on. When the correct node is found, the request goes to the bridge, virtual Ethernet, and, finally, the pod.

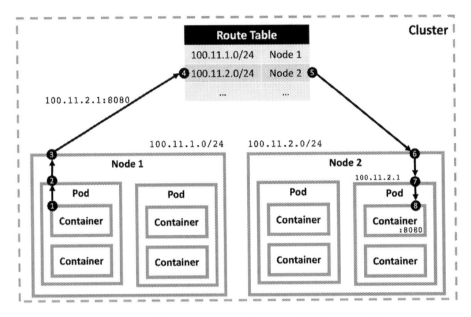

Figure 6-6. *Pod to pod communication on different nodes*

Kubernetes network implementations handle communication between nodes and cluster level. The implementations follow the Container Network Interface (CNI), an open source API specification, and they are installed to clusters as plugins. In the following section, you will learn more about CNI and see it in action.

Container Network Interface (CNI)

Container Network Interface (CNI) is a standard interface definition between network plugins and container runtimes. It is adopted by all significant container orchestrators such as Kubernetes, Mesos, and Cloud Foundry. In addition, various cloud providers such as Amazon ECS, OpenShift, Cisco, and VMware also implement CNI plugins as part of their container platforms. Therefore, developing a new networking plugin following the CNI standard will make you compatible with most of the modern cloud ecosystem.

CNI consists of a JSON-based binary plugin specification, built-in plugins, and libraries to develop custom third-party plugins. CNI team provides and maintains the following built-in plugins under three groups:

- **Main plugins for interface creating:**

    - `bridge` creates a bridge and adds the host and the container to it.

    - `ipvlan` adds an ipvlan interface in the container.

    - `loopback` sets the state of the loopback interface to up.

    - `macvlan` creates a new MAC address and forwards all traffic to the container.

    - `ptp` creates a veth pair.

    - `vlan` allocates a vlan device.

    - `host-device` moves an existing device into a container.

    - `win-bridge` creates a bridge and adds the host and the container to it in Windows-specific environments.

    - `win-overlay` creates an overlay interface to the container in Windows-specific environments.

- **IPAM plugins for IP address allocation:**

    - `dhcp` runs a daemon on the host to make DHCP requests on behalf of the containers.

    - `host-local` maintains a local database of allocated IPs.

    - `static` allocates static IP addresses to containers.

- **Meta and other plugins:**

  - `flannel` generates an interface corresponding to a flannel config file.

  - `tuning` tweaks sysctl parameters of an existing interface.

  - `portmap` maintains an iptables-based port mapping and maps ports from the host to the container.

  - `bandwidth` allows bandwidth limiting.

  - `sbr` configures a source-based routing.

  - `firewall` uses iptables or firewalld to add rules to allow traffic to and from the containers.

CNI focuses on the network connectivity of containers with a plugin-oriented approach. The listed plugins cover fundamental networking operations such as creating a bridge, IP allocation, or connection between host and containers. In addition to built-in plugins, a sample plugin with boilerplate code is maintained to develop custom CNI plugins easily.

Integration of CNI plugins starts with a network configuration in JSON provided to container runtime as diagrammed in Figure 6-7. Then, the runtime calls the CNI executable file with the commands based on the container lifecycle. The plugin runs against the networking infrastructure and connects containers to create the fabric of container orchestration.

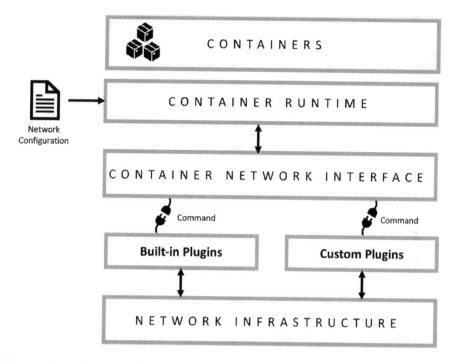

Figure 6-7. *CNI and container runtime integration*

According to the specification, you should implement the following commands:

- ADD command for adding containers to a network

- DEL command for removing containers from networks

- CHECK command for validating connectivity

- VERSION for returning the supported CNI versions

As the commands and expectations are simple in CNI, you can create your plugin in BASH and deploy it as a custom third-party plugin. In the following section, you will learn more about CNI plugins in Kubernetes and their integration.

CNI Plugins in Kubernetes

Kubernetes is the maintainer, the most active contributor, and a keen user of CNI. Kubernetes requires containers reaching other containers living on the same or remote nodes. The network *just* works when you create a Kubernetes cluster in a cloud platform such as GCP, AWS, or Azure. The cloud providers have their CNI plugins installed and configured to work with their infrastructure in the best way. However, when you create an on-prem Kubernetes cluster, you have the freedom of choosing a CNI plugin or developing from scratch.

There are nearly 30 third-party CNI plugins listed in the official repository of containernetworking/cni. Each plugin has its advantages and disadvantages; thus, a comparison is reasonably tricky. However, we can discuss the featured plugins with their essential features:

- Flannel is one of the oldest and most mature plugins, and it comes with a simple and easy way to configure a Layer 3 network fabric. It is responsible for providing and managing the IP network between the nodes of the cluster. It is easy to deploy it to a Kubernetes cluster as it runs as a DaemonSet on each node.

- Weave Net is a simple to use CNI plugin without the requirement of complex configuration or extra code. In addition, Weave Net provides additional features such as DNS, IPAM, and a firewall. You can configure and launch a network fabric using the command-line tool weave.

- Multus is a plugin for Kubernetes to enable attaching multiple network interfaces to pods. By default, each pod in Kubernetes has only an interface; however, multus acts as a metaplugin to call various other CNI plugins. It is configured via CRDs, so it is Kubernetes-native by design.

- Calico is a networking and security solution aimed at
  containers, VMs, and node services. It supports various
  data planes such as a pure Linux eBPF, standard Linux
  networking, or Windows HNS data plane. It provides
  a full networking stack; however, it is common to use
  it in conjunction with other cloud providers, CNIs, to
  provide network policy features.

In the following section, you will see Calico in action by running in a
Kubernetes cluster.

Calico CNI Plugin in Action

By default, minikube provides a single-node Kubernetes cluster with a
basic networking setup. You can enable CNI and install Calico with the
following command.

Listing 6-13. Minikube with Calico

```
$ minikube start --cni=calico
☺ minikube v1.18.0 on Darwin 11.2.2
✦ Automatically selected the docker driver. Other choices:
  hyperkit, ssh
👍 Starting control plane node minikube in cluster minikube
🗄 Downloading Kubernetes v1.20.2 preload ...
🔥 Creating docker container (CPUs=2, Memory=1988MB) ...
🐳 Preparing Kubernetes v1.20.2 on Docker 20.10.3 ...
🔗 Configuring Calico (Container Networking Interface) ...
🔍 Verifying Kubernetes components...
💡 Restarting the docker service may improve performance.
  ▪ Using image gcr.io/k8s-minikube/storage-provisioner:v4
🌟 Enabled addons: storage-provisioner, default-storageclass
🏃 Done! kubectl is now configured to use "minikube" cluster
  and "default" namespace by default
```

In a couple of seconds, the installation will complete, and you can check the Calico pods with the following command.

Listing 6-14. Calico pods

```
$ kubectl -n kube-system get pods -l k8s-app=calico-node
NAME                     READY   STATUS     RESTARTS   AGE
calico-node-p9bjs        1/1     Running    0          4m46s
```

Now, add a second node to minikube and check whether it has connected to the cluster.

Listing 6-15. Adding node to cluster

```
$ minikube node add
☺ Adding node m02 to cluster minikube
🔥 Starting node minikube-m02 in cluster minikube
🐳 Creating docker container (CPUs=2, Memory=2200MB) ...
🏗 Preparing Kubernetes v1.20.2 on Docker 20.10.3 ...
🔎 Verifying Kubernetes components...
🏃 Successfully added m02 to minikube!

$ kubectl get nodes
NAME            STATUS   ROLES                  AGE   VERSION
minikube        Ready    control-plane,master   17m   v1.20.2
minikube-m02    Ready    <none>                 53s   v1.20.2
```

The listing shows two nodes as expected, and it indicates that networking between the nodes is set up successfully. Now, let's deep dive into what has been running and how it is configured.

In every node of the cluster, there should be a Calico application running.

Listing 6-16. DaemonSets in the cluster

```
$ kubectl -n kube-system get daemonsets
NAME            DESIRED  CURRENT  READY  UP-TO-DATE  AVAILABLE
NODE SELECTOR              AGE
calico-node  2           2        2      2           2
kubernetes.io/os=linux   18m
kube-proxy   2           2        2      2           2
kubernetes.io/os=linux   18m
```

Calico should provide the network configuration in JSON format. You can check with the following command in the node.

Listing 6-17. Network configuration in the cluster

```
$ minikube ssh
docker@minikube:~$ cat /etc/cni/net.d/10-calico.conflist
{
  "name": "k8s-pod-network",
  "cniVersion": "0.3.1",
  "plugins": [
   {
     "type": "calico",
     "log_level": "info",
     "datastore_type": "kubernetes",
     "nodename": "minikube",
     "mtu": 1440,
     "ipam": {
       "type": "calico-ipam"
     },
     "policy": {
       "type": "k8s"
     },
```

```
  "kubernetes": {
    "kubeconfig": "/etc/cni/net.d/calico-kubeconfig"
  }
 },
 {
  "type": "portmap",
  "snat": true,
  "capabilities": {"portMappings": true}
 },
 {
  "type": "bandwidth",
  "capabilities": {"bandwidth": true}
 }
 ]
}
```

Finally, it is expected to see the CNI binaries in the host system as CNI plugins follow the binary extension pattern. Let's check the binary folders in the node.

Listing 6-18. CNI binaries

```
docker@minikube:~$ ls /opt/cni/bin/
bandwidth calico    dhcp    flannel    host-local loopback
portmap sbr    tuning vrf
bridge    calico-ipam firewall host-device
ipvlan    macvlan ptp    static vlan
```

With the Calico installation, CNI plugins and configuration are deployed to the Kubernetes nodes. If you need to extend the networking capabilities of Kubernetes by configuring, installing, or developing CNI plugins, you need to follow the same pattern. It is worth mentioning the following three points if you plan to build your own CNI plugins:

- **Scalability**: Networking is both the bottleneck and opportunity when it comes to scalability. You can find yourself limited by the complexity and overhead of networking topology while scaling up your nodes. Therefore, you need to design your CNI plugin based on the cluster's expected number of nodes.

- **Infrastructure Limits**: Most of the CNI plugins are developed to overcome an infrastructure limit by creating solutions in the upper layers. Know the boundaries and barriers in your computing and networking infrastructure and design your CNI plugins accordingly.

- **Complexity vs. Feature Set**: When you look at the available third-party CNI plugins, you will be overwhelmed with the provided features. It is suggested to start small by giving the must-have features first. For instance, if you do not expect to work with network policies, you can eliminate this feature while designing your CNI plugin.

In the following section, device plugins will be discussed as the third and last infrastructure extension point of Kubernetes.

Device Plugins

Kubernetes workloads run on the nodes and consume the resources. The resources on the nodes can be CPU, memory, storage, or any custom device provided by vendors such as GPUs, high-performance NICs, or FPGAs. Since it is not feasible to cover all vendors and devices as a resource in the source code, Kubernetes provides a device plugin framework. The framework is the extension point to advertise and allocate

213

system hardware resources via kubelet. Instead of customizing the code, vendors implement their plugins and deploy them to the cluster to extend the resource allocation mechanism of Kubernetes.

In this section, you will learn about the device plugin API and lifecycle. In addition, you will develop a device plugin from scratch and deploy it to the cluster to see it in action.

Device Plugin API

Device plugins are applications running on the node and communicating with the kubelet. Therefore, they follow the binary plugin extension pattern. The entry point is the registration into kubelet with the provided gRPC service.

Listing 6-19. kubelet registration service

```
service Registration {
    rpc Register(RegisterRequest) returns (Empty) {}
}
```

In the registration, the plugin sends the following information to the kubelet Unix socket located at /var/lib/kubelet/device-plugins/kubelet.sock:

- Name of the device plugin socket

- Device plugin API version

- Resource name in the extended resource naming scheme such as vendor-domain/resource-type

After the registration, the device plugin is responsible for serving a gRPC service with a Unix socket located at /var/lib/kubelet/device-plugins/. The service implements the following interface.

Listing 6-20. Device plugin interface

```
service DevicePlugin {
    rpc GetDevicePluginOptions(Empty) returns
    (DevicePluginOptions) {}
    rpc ListAndWatch(Empty) returns (stream
    ListAndWatchResponse) {}
    rpc Allocate(AllocateRequest) returns
    (AllocateResponse) {}
    rpc GetPreferredAllocation(PreferredAllocationRequest)
    returns (PreferredAllocationResponse) {}
    rpc PreStartContainer(PreStartContainerRequest) returns
    (PreStartContainerResponse) {}
}
```

- GetDevicePluginOptions is the metafunction to provide information about the plugin.

- ListAndWatch is the function that runs continuously and streams the updated list of devices.

- Allocate is the essential function called during the container creation. The device plugin handles infrastructure-related preparation operations. Then, it returns parameters to make devices available to containers.

- GetPreferredAllocation and PreStartContainer functions are optional functions.

The pods request the custom device plugin resources as part of their container specification. For instance, if the device plugin advertises that there are ten instances of extend-k8s.io/custom-resource available on the node, then Kubernetes API uses this information on node status and scheduling decisions. The following pod definition requires three

215

instances of the extend-k8s.io/custom-resource device. Kubernetes will only schedule the pod to a node if there are enough resources to satisfy the need.

Listing 6-21. Pod with custom device resource

```
apiVersion: v1
kind: Pod
metadata:
  name: example-pod
spec:
  containers:
    - name: example-container
      image: k8s.gcr.io/pause:2.0
      resources:
        limits:
          extend-k8s.io/custom-resource: 3
```

Device plugins should be available on Kubernetes nodes and more specifically in /var/lib/kubelet/device-plugins folders. Therefore, you need to either install them manually or deploy them as a DaemonSet in the cluster. DaemonSets have additional advantages such as automated upgrades and restarting the plugins after kubelet failures.

There are already a couple of device plugin implementations in the cloud-native ecosystem. These are the open source plugins that are created and maintained by vendors:

- AMD GPU device plugin

- NVIDIA GPU device plugin

- Intel device plugins for GPU, FPGA, QAT, VPU, SGX, and DSA devices

- KubeVirt device plugins for hardware-assisted virtualization

- RDMA device plugin

- Solarflare device plugin

- SR-IOV Network device plugin

- Xilinx FPGA device plugins

In the following section, you will create an example device plugin and deploy it to a cluster.

Development and Deployment of a Device Plugin

Let's start by creating a cluster with the following command: `minikube start --kubernetes-version v1.19.0`.

Then, create the following folder structure in your Go environment.

Listing 6-22. Go project initialization

```
$ mkdir -p $GOPATH/src/extend-k8s.io/k8s-device-plugin-example
$ cd $GOPATH/src/extend-k8s.io/k8s-device-plugin-example
$ mkdir -p cmd pkg
```

Create a `main.go` file in `cmd` folder with the following content.

Listing 6-23. Main file for device plugin

```
package main

import (
        "flag"

        "github.com/kubevirt/device-plugin-manager/pkg/dpm"
        "github.com/extend-k8s.io/k8s-device-plugin-example/pkg"
)
```

```go
func main() {
        flag.Parse()
        manager := dpm.NewManager(pkg.Lister{})
        manager.Run()
}
```

It is a very simple main function to create a new manager using the Lister. Now, let's create a lister.go file in the pkg folder with the following content.

Listing 6-24. Lister implementation

```go
package pkg

import (
        "github.com/kubevirt/device-plugin-manager/pkg/dpm"
)

type Lister struct{}

func (Lister) GetResourceNamespace() string {
        return "extend-k8s.io"
}

func (Lister) Discover(pluginListCh chan dpm.PluginNameList) {

        pluginListCh <- dpm.PluginNameList{"example"}
}

func (Lister) NewPlugin(deviceID string) dpm.PluginInterface {
        return &ExamplePlugin{}
}
```

It is used in the registration and discovery of the device plugin with the extend-k8s.io/example name. In addition, it returns a PluginInterface that you will implement next.

Create a plugin.go file in pkg folder with the following content.

Listing 6-25. Plugin implementation

```
package pkg

import (
        "context"
        "math/rand"
        "time"

        "github.com/thanhpk/randstr"

        . "k8s.io/kubelet/pkg/apis/deviceplugin/v1beta1"
)

type ExamplePlugin struct{}

func (dp *ExamplePlugin) ListAndWatch(e *Empty, s DevicePlugin_
ListAndWatchServer) error {

        s.Send(&ListAndWatchResponse{Devices: randomDevices()})

        for {
                time.Sleep(5 * time.Second)
                s.Send(&ListAndWatchResponse{Devices:
                randomDevices()})
        }
}
func (dp *ExamplePlugin) Allocate(c context.Context, r
*AllocateRequest) (*AllocateResponse, error) {

        envs := map[string]string{"K8S_DEVICE_PLUGIN_EXAMPLE":
        randstr.Hex(16)}
        responses := []*ContainerAllocateResponse{{Envs: envs}}
```

```go
        return &AllocateResponse{ContainerResponses: responses},
        nil
}

func (ExamplePlugin) GetDevicePluginOptions(context.Context,
*Empty) (*DevicePluginOptions, error) {
        return nil, nil
}

func (ExamplePlugin) PreStartContainer(context.Context,
*PreStartContainerRequest) (*PreStartContainerResponse, error)
{
        return nil, nil
}

func (dp *ExamplePlugin) GetPreferredAllocation(context.
Context, *PreferredAllocationRequest)
(*PreferredAllocationResponse, error) {
        return nil, nil
}

func randomDevices() []*Device {

        devices := make([]*Device, 0)
        for i := 0; i < rand.Intn(5)+1; i++ {
                devices = append(devices, &Device{
                        ID:      randstr.Hex(16),
                        Health: Healthy,
                })
        }

        return devices
}
```

The file has two important points to mention:

- ListAndWatch function starts by registering a set of random devices. Then it updates the devices every 5 seconds with a new set of random devices.

- Allocate function returns an environment variable K8S_DEVICE_PLUGIN_EXAMPLE to be passed to the containers. This approach is helpful to use custom devices in your applications.

Create a go.mod file in the root folder of the project with the following content.

Listing 6-26. Dependency file

```
module github.com/extend-k8s.io/k8s-device-plugin-example

go 1.14

require (
        github.com/kubevirt/device-plugin-manager v1.18.8
        github.com/thanhpk/randstr v1.0.4
        k8s.io/kubelet v0.19.0
)
```

Finally, create a Dockerfile with the following two-layered approach.

Listing 6-27. Dockerfile for device plugin

```
FROM golang:1.14-alpine as builder
ADD . /go/src/github.com/extend-k8s.io/k8s-device-plugin-
example
WORKDIR /go/src/github.com/extend-k8s.io/k8s-device-plugin-
example/cmd
RUN go build -v
```

```
FROM alpine:latest
COPY --from=builder /go/src/github.com/extend-k8s.io/k8s-
device-plugin-example/cmd/cmd /usr/local/bin/k8s-device-plugin-
example
CMD ["k8s-device-plugin-example"]
```

Now, you can build and deploy the Docker image of the device plugin with the following commands.

Note   Set DOCKER_REPOSITORY environment variable according to your Docker repository.

Listing 6-28. Container build

```
$ docker build -t $DOCKER_REPOSITORY/k8s-device-plugin-
example:v1 .

=> [internal] load build definition from Dockerfile
...
naming to docker.io/$DOCKER_REPOSITORY/k8s-device-plugin-
example:v1

$  docker push $DOCKER_REPOSITORY/k8s-device-plugin-example:v1

The push refers to repository [docker.io/$DOCKER_REPOSITORY/
k8s-device-plugin-example]
...
v1: digest: sha256:91e41..bffc size: 739
```

Deploy the plugin to the cluster using the following DaemonSet definition.

Note   Do not forget to change `DOCKER_REPOSITORY` to the environment variable.

Listing 6-29. DaemonSet for device plugin

```
apiVersion: apps/v1
kind: DaemonSet
metadata:
  labels:
    name: device-plugin-example
  name: device-plugin-example
  namespace: kube-system
spec:
  selector:
    matchLabels:
      name: device-plugin-example
  template:
    metadata:
      labels:
        name: device-plugin-example
    spec:
      containers:
      - name: device-plugin-example
        image: $DOCKER_REPOSITORY/k8s-device-plugin-example:v1
        securityContext:
          privileged: true
        volumeMounts:
          - name: device-plugin
            mountPath: /var/lib/kubelet/device-plugins
      volumes:
```

```
      - name: device-plugin
        hostPath:
          path: /var/lib/kubelet/device-plugins
```

Check and ensure the device plugin pod is running.

Listing 6-30. Pod listing

```
$ kubectl -n kube-system get pods -l name=device-plugin-example
NAME                          READY   STATUS    RESTARTS   AGE
device-plugin-example-bgktv   1/1     Running   0          2m6s
```

You can check the status of custom devices from the node status data.

Listing 6-31. Device information in the node status

```
$ kubectl get node minikube -w -o json | jq '.status.
allocatable."extend-k8s.io/example"'
"3"
"2"
"1"
"2"
```

The command watches for the nodes and prints only the custom device information. Since the device plugin updates with a random number of devices, you should see changes similar to the preceding one. It shows that the device plugin is configured correctly and interacts with kubelet to set node status. You can stop the watch command and return to the terminal via CTRL+C.

Now, let's create a pod to use the custom device with the following content.

Listing 6-32. Pod with custom device

```
apiVersion: v1
kind: Pod
metadata:
  name: device-plugin-consumer
spec:
  containers:
  - name: pause
    image: busybox
    command: ["/bin/sleep", "1000"]
    resources:
      limits:
        extend-k8s.io/example: 1
```

When the pod is running, execute the following command to check environment variables.

Listing 6-33. Container environment variables

```
$ kubectl exec device-plugin-consumer -- env

PATH=/usr/local/sbin:/usr/local/bin:/usr/sbin:/usr/bin:/sbin:/
bin
HOSTNAME=device-plugin-consumer
K8S_DEVICE_PLUGIN_EXAMPLE=5a1b85e33a06f47501504a9c570e4e32
KUBERNETES_PORT_443_TCP_ADDR=10.96.0.1
KUBERNETES_SERVICE_HOST=10.96.0.1
KUBERNETES_SERVICE_PORT=443
KUBERNETES_SERVICE_PORT_HTTPS=443
KUBERNETES_PORT=tcp://10.96.0.1:443
KUBERNETES_PORT_443_TCP=tcp://10.96.0.1:443
```

```
KUBERNETES_PORT_443_TCP_PROTO=tcp
KUBERNETES_PORT_443_TCP_PORT=443
HOME=/root
```

The environment variables list shows that K8S_DEVICE_PLUGIN_ EXAMPLE passed from the device plugin to kubelet and injected into the container. The last step complements the flow of a device plugin approach from the gRPC server to the container.

Creating and running device plugins are straightforward compared to storage and networking plugins. Device plugin API is moderately new and has not a full-fledged standard similar to CSI and CNI. Therefore, it is essential to check API changes and Kubernetes version compatibility during device plugins' development.

Key Takeaways

- Kubernetes is an open ecosystem and does not restrict any cloud provider or on-prem system.

- Interaction of Kubernetes with the infrastructure layer is extendible with storage, network, and device plugins.

- Storage plugins extend the volume provisioning in Kubernetes while implementing the CSI standard.

- Networking plugins extend the container networking in the cluster while implementing the CNI standard.

- Device plugins extend the resource allocation and usage of custom devices by vendors.

In the following chapter, we will discuss the upcoming trends, platforms, and libraries in the Kubernetes world.

CHAPTER 7

Upcoming Extension Points

Keep your eyes on the stars, and your feet on the ground.

—Theodore Roosevelt
The 26th President of the United States

Kubernetes is a proven success with its strong foundation in the cloud-native world. It provides a rich set of features to manage containerized applications and various extension points to add new capabilities. Nevertheless, Kubernetes is not a finished project; it is probably the most active open source project in the software development history. Thus, this very last chapter will focus on the upcoming trends, extension points, and libraries for Kubernetes. At the end of this chapter, you will learn more about the latest developments and future trends in the Kubernetes world. The bright future of Kubernetes will increase your excitement, and you will be happy to be a part of this journey to the stars.

In this very last chapter, two upcoming extension points that are still in development will be covered. Let's start with the Service Catalog extension API to enable applications running in Kubernetes to use external managed services.

© Onur Yilmaz 2021
O. Yilmaz, *Extending Kubernetes*, https://doi.org/10.1007/978-1-4842-7095-0_7

Service Catalog

The Service Catalog is the extension point in Kubernetes to open its doors to other managed services. It enables applications running in the cluster to use external software operated by a cloud provider. Let's assume you have a Kubernetes cluster and an application that needs a message queue. You have basically two options: deploy a message queue into your cluster or use message queue service from your cloud provider. The first option is very flexible, but it comes with its operational burden. You need to find a *bridge* between the Kubernetes cluster and the cloud provider's message queue service for the latter option. The bridge is Service Catalog with the following architecture in Figure 7-1.

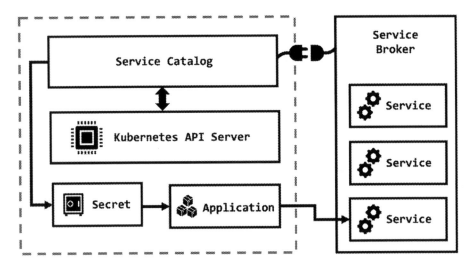

Figure 7-1. *Service Catalog overview*

Service Catalog extends Kubernetes API by listing managed services, provisioning an instance, and binding into an application running inside the cluster. External services are connected to the cluster using *service broker* endpoints defined by the Open Service Broker API.

On the Kubernetes API side, the Service Catalog installs an extension API server and a controller to manage the following API resources under `servicecatalog.k8s.io` group:

- **ClusterServiceBroker**: It is the definition of a service broker with its connection details. Cluster admins install new brokers using `ClusterServiceBroker` resources.

- **ClusterServiceClass**: It is the managed service provided by `ClusterServiceBroker`. When a new `ClusterServiceBroker` is added to the cluster, the Service Catalog connects to the broker and retrieves the list of managed services to create corresponding `ClusterServiceClass` resources.

- **ClusterServicePlan**: It describes specific offerings of `ClusterServiceClass`, such as free tier, paid tier, or particular versions. `ClusterServicePlan` resources are created by Service Catalog just after a new broker is installed.

- **ServiceInstance**: It is a provisioned instance of `ClusterServiceClass`. When you need a new instance of the managed service, you need to create a `ServiceInstance`. Then, the Service Catalog controller connects to the service broker and provisions a service instance.

- **ServiceBinding**: It is the access credentials to use `ServiceInstance` in your application in the cluster. When you create a new `ServiceBinding`, the Service Catalog creates a secret with the connection details to the `ServiceInstance`. You can mount the secret into your application and connect to the external managed service.

API resources and Service Catalog controllers ensure that external managed services and plans are available in the cluster. In addition, it enables creating new instances of services and binding to the applications running in the cluster. In the following exercise, you will see Service Catalog in action and extend Kubernetes cluster with managed applications.

EXERCISE 1: SERVICE CATALOG IN ACTION

In this exercise, you will walk through all Service Catalog capabilities and see how it extends Kubernetes. You will first deploy the Service Catalog to the cluster, install a service broker, and finally create some managed services.

Note   The rest of the exercise is based on deploying resources to the cluster, and it requires the following prerequisites: `minikube`, `kubectl`, and `helm`.

---

1. Create a Kubernetes cluster using minikube with the following command: `minikube start --kubernetes-version v1.19.0`.

2. Service Catalog has a Helm chart to be installed. Thus, you need to add its chart repository first and then install it with the following commands:

    ```
    $ helm repo add svc-cat https://kubernetes-sigs.github.
    io/service-catalog
    "svc-cat" has been added to your repositories

    $ kubectl create namespace catalog
    namespace/catalog created
    $ helm install catalog svc-cat/catalog --namespace
    catalog
    ```

```
..
NAME: catalog
LAST DEPLOYED: ...
NAMESPACE: catalog
STATUS: deployed
REVISION: 1
TEST SUITE: None
```

Commands install the Service Catalog API resources and controllers. You can see the list of custom resources with the following command:

```
$ kubectl get crd | grep servicecatalog.k8s.io
clusterservicebrokers.servicecatalog.k8s.io
clusterserviceclasses.servicecatalog.k8s.io
clusterserviceplans.servicecatalog.k8s.io
servicebindings.servicecatalog.k8s.io
servicebrokers.servicecatalog.k8s.io
serviceclasses.servicecatalog.k8s.io
serviceinstances.servicecatalog.k8s.io
serviceplans.servicecatalog.k8s.io
```

3. You need to install a service broker to manage third-party applications, and it must have Open Service Broker API to interact with the Service Catalog. There is already a service broker to work in minikube named minibroker, and you can deploy it with the following commands:

```
$ helm repo add minibroker https://minibroker.blob.core.
windows.net/charts
"minibroker" has been added to your repositories

$ kubectl create namespace minibroker
namespace/minibroker created
```

```
$ helm install minibroker minibroker/minibroker
--namespace minibroker
NAME: minibroker
LAST DEPLOYED: Fri Mar 26 12:21:27 2021
NAMESPACE: minibroker
STATUS: deployed
REVISION: 1
TEST SUITE: None
```

4. Service Catalog controller creates `ClusterServiceClass` for each service that the broker provides. You can list the provided services with the following command:

```
$ kubectl get clusterserviceclasses
NAME            EXTERNAL-NAME   BROKER       AGE
mariadb         mariadb         minibroker   3m
mongodb         mongodb         minibroker   3m
mysql           mysql           minibroker   3m
postgresql      postgresql      minibroker   3m
rabbitmq        rabbitmq        minibroker   3m
redis           redis           minibroker   3m
```

The broker service deployed in Step 3 provides the preceding listed services. In addition, these services should have plans as follows:

```
$ kubectl get clusterserviceplans
NAME              EXTERNAL-NAME   BROKER       CLASS     AGE
mariadb-10-1-26   10-1-26         minibroker   mariadb   9m
...
mongodb-3-4-10    3-4-10          minibroker   mongodb   8m
...
```

mysql-5-7-30	5-7-30	minibroker	mysql	8m
...				
postgresql-9-6-2	9-6-2	minibroker	postgresql	8m
...				
rabbitmq-3-6-10	3-6-10	minibroker	rabbitmq	8m
...				
redis-5-0-7	5-0-7	minibroker	redis	8m

The long list consists of every preconfigured plan of the services available in the broker.

5. Now, it is time to create some managed database instances. Create a ServiceInstance resource with the following content into a file named db-instance.yaml and deploy it to the cluster:

```
apiVersion: servicecatalog.k8s.io/v1beta1
kind: ServiceInstance
metadata:
  name: db-instance
  namespace: test-db
spec:
  clusterServiceClassExternalName: mysql
  clusterServicePlanExternalName: 5-7-30
```

```
$ kubectl create namespace test-db
namespace/test-db created
```

```
$ kubectl apply -f db-instance.yaml
serviceinstance.servicecatalog.k8s.io/db-instance created
```

Wait for a couple of seconds, and your database instance will
be Ready:

```
$ kubectl get serviceinstances -n test-db
NAME          CLASS                         PLAN    STATUS AGE
db-instance   ClusterServiceClass/mysql   5-7-30   Ready  2m53s
```

6. Create a ServiceBinding resource to use the managed
   database in your applications. When the ServiceBinding
   resource is created, the Service Catalog controller will connect
   to the broker and retrieve connection details and credentials.
   Create a ServiceBinding with the following content and into
   a file named db-binding.yaml:

```
apiVersion: servicecatalog.k8s.io/v1beta1
kind: ServiceBinding
metadata:
 name: db-binding
 namespace: test-db
spec:
 instanceRef:
  name: db-instance
```

```
$ kubectl apply -f db-binding.yaml
servicebinding.servicecatalog.k8s.io/db-binding created
```

In a couple of seconds, the connection information and
credentials will be collected into a secret resource as follows:

```
$ kubectl -n test-db describe secret db-binding
Name:      db-binding
Namespace: test-db
Labels:    <none>
Annotations: <none>
```

```
Type: Opaque

Data
====
database:          0 bytes
mysql-password:    10 bytes
password:          10 bytes
username:          4 bytes
uri:            81 bytes
host:           52 bytes
mysql-root-password: 10 bytes
port:           4 bytes
protocol:       5 bytes
```

7. Create a pod for connecting to the database and using credentials from the secret. Use the following content and save into a file named my-app.yaml:

```
apiVersion: v1
kind: Pod
metadata:
  name: my-app
  namespace: test-db
spec:
  containers:
  - name: app
    image: mysql
    command: ["bash"]
    args: ["-c", "sleep infinity"]
    env:
      - name: MYSQL_HOST
        valueFrom:
          secretKeyRef:
            name: db-binding
            key: host
```

```
        - name: MYSQL_TCP_PORT
          valueFrom:
            secretKeyRef:
              name: db-binding
              key: port
        - name: MYSQL_USER
          valueFrom:
            secretKeyRef:
              name: db-binding
              key: username
        - name: MYSQL_PASSWORD
          valueFrom:
            secretKeyRef:
              name: db-binding
              key: password
    restartPolicy: Never
```

```
$ kubectl apply -f  my-app.yaml
pod/my-app created
```

8. Wait until the test-db pod is in Running state and then connect to the pod and execute MySQL commands to validate managed database application:

```
$ kubectl exec -n test-db my-app -it -- bash
```

```
root@my-app:/# mysql -u$MYSQL_USER -p$MYSQL_PASSWORD -e
"select version()"
mysql: [Warning] Using a password on the command line
interface can be insecure.
+-----------+
| version() |
+-----------+
| 5.7.30    |
+-----------+
```

It shows that the application running in the Kubernetes cluster can connect to the database and run queries. The connection information and credentials are provided from the secret created by the Service Catalog.

9. You can clean the resources and installations with the following commands:

```
$ kubectl delete namespace test-db
$ kubectl delete servicebinding db-binding
$ kubectl delete serviceinstances test-db
$ kubectl delete clusterservicebrokers minibroker
$ helm delete --purge minibroker
$ kubectl delete namespace minibroker
$ helm delete --purge catalog
$ kubectl delete namespace catalog
```

In the previous exercise, all aspects of the Service Catalog extension are covered. You have started with the installation of Service Catalog API resources and controllers. Then, a service broker is installed following Open Service Broker API. Following that, a managed database instance is created and connected from an application running in the Kubernetes cluster. The Service Catalog extends the Kubernetes for managing external applications and employing them inside the cluster. It creates a strong connection between the applications running inside and outside the cluster.

In order to extend Kubernetes with Service Catalog, you need to develop and run service brokers for your third-party external applications. Service Catalog API and controllers will make them integrated into the cluster so that applications in the cluster can connect and consume.

Next, extending Kubernetes API to provision, upgrade, and operate multiple Kubernetes clusters will be covered.

Cluster API

Cluster API is the Kubernetes-native way of providing a declarative API to provision, upgrade, and operate Kubernetes clusters. In other words, it is the extension point for Kubernetes to manage Kubernetes clusters. Kubernetes clusters and infrastructure such as virtual machines, networks, storage, or load balancers can be defined as any other Kubernetes-native resources such as deployments or pods. Platform operators running in the clusters automate the lifecycle of clusters and underlying infrastructure. This approach's main advantage is repeatable and consistent cluster management across different cloud or infrastructure providers.

Running a Kubernetes cluster is not straightforward as it requires multiple components to be configured correctly. It is a high entry to barrier for new starters in the Kubernetes ecosystem. In addition, there are more than 60 Kubernetes certified distributions and installers with their configuration and style. kubeadm is the response from the Kubernetes community to bootstrap clusters following the best practices. Although kubeadm solves the complexity of the cluster installation, it does not address the cluster lifecycle management. Cluster API is the solution to fill the gaps related to day-to-day cluster management operations, such as provisioning the new VMs, load balancers, and automation. Cluster API creates an extension point in Kubernetes API to define and manage Kubernetes clusters declaratively. You can connect to any infrastructure or cloud system to provision resources or bootstrap provider to install Kubernetes control plane.

There are two types of clusters in Cluster API:

- **Workload cluster** is the Kubernetes cluster to be managed via Cluster API.

- **Management cluster** manages the lifecycle of Workload
  Clusters with the installed providers. Management clusters
  have Cluster API CRDs and follow the controller pattern to
  manage the lifecycle of workload clusters.

Two types of providers manage the lifecycle of workload clusters:

- **Infrastructure providers** are responsible for creating
  infrastructure resources such as compute, storage, and
  networking.

- **Bootstrap providers** are responsible for installing the
  Kubernetes control plane and joining worker nodes to
  the cluster.

The relationship between providers and the clusters can be
summarized as follows in Figure 7-2.

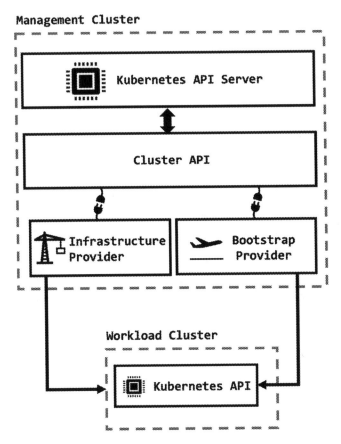

Figure 7-2. *Cluster API overview*

You can extend Kubernetes cluster management using Cluster API
with two extension points: *adding new infrastructure providers* and *adding
new bootstrap providers.* You can add new infrastructure providers to
create bare metal nodes, VMs, or any other virtualized instances based on
your custom requirements. Similarly, you can develop and deploy new
bootstrap providers to implement custom requirements for Kubernetes
internal operations. However, as the Cluster API resources and controllers
are actively updated, you should check the latest reference documentation
and The Cluster API Book.

Key Takeaways

- Kubernetes is not a finished product; it is in an active development stage.

- There are still extension points that are in development to extend Kubernetes further.

- Service Catalog is the extension point to incorporate external services into the cluster.

- Cluster API provides a declarative API to manage the lifecycle of other Kubernetes clusters.

Conclusion

Kubernetes is a complex container orchestrator with its extension points, and this book has covered all available extension points by grouping them on their functionality and underlying extension patterns. In each chapter, you have learned the extension points from a technical perspective and got your hands dirty. With the information and experience you have gained throughout the book, I hope you will be more ambitious about the future of Kubernetes and how you will extend the Kubernetes to enrich its ecosystem.

Index

© Onur Yilmaz 2021
O. Yilmaz, *Extending Kubernetes*, https://doi.org/10.1007/978-1-4842-7095-0